# Relationship Skills in Social Work

Roger Hennessey

Los Angeles | London | New Delhi
Singapore | Washington DC

SAGE Publications Ltd
1 Oliver's Yard
55 City Road
London EC1Y 1SP

SAGE Publications Inc.
2455 Teller Road
Thousand Oaks, California 91320

SAGE Publications India Pvt Ltd
B 1/I 1 Mohan Cooperative Industrial Area
Mathura Road
New Delhi 110 044

SAGE Publications Asia-Pacific Pte Ltd
33 Pekin Street #02-01
Far East Square
Singapore 048763

Library of Congress Control Number: 2010929655

British Library Cataloguing in Publication data

A catalogue record for this book is available from the British Library

ISBN 978-1-84860-155-0
ISBN 978-1-84860-156-7 (pbk)

Typeset by C&M Digitals (P) Ltd, Chennai, India
Printed by CPI Antony Rowe, Chippenham, Wiltshire
Printed on paper from sustainable resources

MIX
Paper from
responsible sources
FSC
www.fsc.org   FSC® C013604

# CONTENTS

# ABOUT THE AUTHOR

Roger Hennessey lives in a rural part of Norfolk. On leaving university a chance meeting caused him to abandon other career plans and start work in a children's home – leading to him training in social work at the University of East Anglia. While there he undertook an extended placement at Peper Harow – then a therapeutic community for adolescent boys in Surrey. The experience was formative in his thinking because in the community it was the understanding and practising of relationships that lay at the heart of constructive outcomes. There it was a form of love rather than sanction which exercised control – an approach to managing behaviour that taught and motivated residents to manage themselves in more constructive ways. On qualifying in social work he returned to residential childcare and, later, became a child and family social worker and guardian *ad litem*. Since the mid-1980s he has taught part time at the School of Social Work and Psychology at UEA and worked part-time as a counsellor in the Norwich diocese, where he also undertakes safeguarding work. His hobbies include riding and repairing his Royal Enfield, maintaining his bicycles and, most of all, cycling through Norfolk lanes and visiting its medieval churches. A few years ago he rode his bike to Santiago de Compostela and he is planning to ride from Canterbury to Rome.

# 1 INTRODUCTION TO RELATIONSHIPS IN SOCIAL WORK

Social work is carried out within a network of human relationships. Indeed, it is human relationships and the many types of problems associated with them that are usually at the root of social workers' professional tasks. And it is this relational dimension in social work practice which often draws students into making it their career – fulfilling their wish to 'work with people'.

This book is an attempt to consider in depth the place of relationships in social work practice and to explore ways in which workers can use relationships to promote creative outcomes in their encounters with clients. As you work through the book you will see why using relationships requires social workers to *use themselves*, and why using the self, in the sense meant here, requires an enhanced knowledge of the self that is being used. So, *self-awareness* in the social worker is a major theme that you will find recurring throughout the chapters.

But first it is essential to understand that social workers' relationships with their clients are not neutral and free-floating. Rather, they are to a greater or lesser extent tied down, influenced and shaped by wider socio-economic, political and cultural contexts. There is no one-to-one relationship between a social worker and a client that is not impacted upon by macro-frameworks such as legislation, or protocol, or departmental budgets. Equally, any specific worker–client relationship will take place within a cultural context that holds particular attitudes towards fundamental dimensions of life such as sexual relationships, child-rearing practices, roles associated with gender, lesbianism and homosexuality, marriage and divorce, and so on.

To these influences on the worker–client relationship must be added the fact that individual social workers are employed by agencies that have specific tasks which will influence any relational interaction a worker has with a client. Thus, the term 'social worker' is multifarious, describing a heterogeneous group of individuals who are employed in settings that may range from statutory work with children to local voluntary agencies with a focus on homelessness or hospice care. And within this diversity of social work roles can be found jobs that are mainly desk-based, working with computerised data, and other work where frequent face-to-face contact with clients is normal and essential to the agency's function. Thus, to begin to understand a specific worker's relationship with a specific client, one would need to know about the macro-structures under which the agency operates, the cultural contexts of the client, the agency's defined tasks and the methods it uses to complete them.

Contextualising worker–client relations is important to understanding them and in the book there are case examples for you to consider in terms of the influences which impinge on the relationship. But in normal circumstances the greatest influence on relationships is workers themselves. It is their *self* which they bring to their relationships and which forms the client's most direct experience of the humanity of social work. The self of the social worker is the 'face' of their agency, and it can be the face that is associated with laws, powers and procedures. Thus the social worker's self is a visible sign and experience for the client of other, less tangible things. It is therefore not surprising that a worker's self and how they use it to relate to their clients can have a huge impact on how the client feels and how they act and react. This is why one important focus in this book is *you*, and how you can learn to develop and use your self creatively and consciously in your professional practice.

In order to help you to develop the skills of using your self the book will provide you with knowledge about the importance of relationships to human well-being, and help you to learn and practise ways of relating that are deeper and more therapeutic. The chapters focus on two basic questions which are the *why* and the *how* of relating. The first question about *why* requires dipping into the theory of relationships and drawing upon the disciplines of psychology, sociology and neuroscience. Each of these in its own way points to the critical impact that relationships have upon the mental, social and physical health of people. And the second question, *how*, is one about techniques and practice skills. Throughout the chapters you will find case studies and exercises that will help you to answer these questions of *why* and *how* and, if you work your way through these on your own and with others, you should make progress towards becoming more confident and competent to use your self as a resource in your professional role.

Though the case studies in the book concern individuals in unique circumstances, and the self-awareness exercises focus upon your individuality, much of the theoretical basis of the book will, by necessity, deal with those dimensions of human experience that are more universal – qualities that remain more or less the same wherever and whenever they are found. And so, as you reflect on your own unique life, you should be able to locate your uniqueness within the more general relational needs and experiences of humankind.

Likewise, the book sets examples of specific worker–client relationships within what appear to be general relational needs. And while frequent reference is made to the National Occupational Standards (NOS) for social work, the standards that are highlighted are those which tend to express relatively constant social work skills and values with regard to worker–client relationships. In doing this, no attempt is being made to deny the relativity of human experience or the changes which it undergoes. Nor is it trying to assert human absolutes by disregarding cultural variation. Rather, it is following in the tradition of humanistic psychology pioneered by Maslow (1968) and Rogers (1980).

Maslow (1968: 3), writing of human need, argues that 'We have, each of us, an essential biologically based inner nature, which is to some degree "natural", intrinsic, given, and in a certain limited sense, unchangeable, or, at least, unchanging'. Here, the claim is that human 'nature', with its needs for safety and security, for belonging, for loving and being loved, for feeling trusted and trusting, has a universal quality that transcends the specificity of any one time, ethnicity or culture.

In like vein, Carl Rogers based his whole professional life on the claim that if we relate to others in ways that are warm, genuine and empathic, then we activate the other person's 'actualising tendency', engaging with them in what he describes as 'an underlying flow of movement toward constructive fulfilment of...inherent possibilities' (1980: 117) in the person. For him, this actualising tendency was at the core of the individual person and was *inherent* – a universal given in the human condition that would thrive if it met relationships that facilitated it, or wither away if it experienced neglect, indifference or abuse. In Rogers the idea is again expressed that the *essence* of humanity is universal, though the form it takes will be influenced by cultural mores, customs, and so on.

This book is written in that humanistic spirit. Though its focus is on social work, what it expresses about human relationships and their capacity to promote, diminish, or even destroy well-being, extends far beyond social work practice. When, as a social worker, you respond with love towards a specific individual you are also responding at the same time to a general need in humanity. In this sense relational social work is part of a much larger picture about human relationships and the qualities within them that can sometimes help others to feel more safe, more trusting and thriving.

## ANTI-OPPRESSION, ANTI-DISCRIMINATION AND RELATIONSHIPS

As you read the book you will find relatively few *explicit* references to anti-oppressive and anti-discriminatory practice, or to principles such as equality, worth, human rights and dignity (though there are references to other sources where these crucial concerns for social work theory and practice are discussed). The reason for this is that, though these principles and attitudes are enshrined in law and protocol, they can, in the final analysis, only ever be expressed meaningfully in human relationships. In other words, it is *only* relationships that can move them beyond being an idea in print and turn them into an experienced reality. The ideas and the practical exercises in the book, when followed, will lead to worker–client relationships that are respectful of culture, age, gender, sexuality – and the many other dimensions of human life in relation to which the social work profession has pioneered tolerance, anti-discrimination and anti-oppression. Thus, while anti-oppressive and anti-discriminatory practices are not explicit, they are enmeshed with most of what is written in this book.

## CLIENTS' VIEWS ABOUT RELATIONSHIPS

The book is written in the belief that many clients want their social workers to relate to them in ways that go beyond a technique-based engagement, however competent that might be in achieving an outcome. For example, research (GSCC 2008) among social workers' clients reveals that

> People using services highlight the importance of the relationship they have with a social worker as key to the positives they associate with social work practice. It is this relationship which is the starting point for building trust and supporting people's self-empowerment. People refer to the strengths of the informality, flexibility and warmth of this relationship.

The qualitative aspects of the relationship that are identified here will be discussed in the chapters that follow. Similar expressions of a need for relationship follow throughout the client groups. For example, quoting from *About Social Workers: A Children's Views Report* the GSCC (2008) writes that

> Social workers need to understand more from a child's perspective about any situation … [they need] understanding of a person's feelings and to understand all children are different … With children in care, they need to always know they have someone they can turn to and talk to … You just want people to listen, understand and be there on a regular basis.

It should go without saying that children in care have usually had prior experience of inconstancy in their relationships, and their relational development will only be enhanced by continuity and consistency from those responsible for looking after them. Social workers cannot provide this unless they are available for the longer term, unless they listen and engage, and try to build trust in children who, for well-understood reasons, are distrustful.

Similarly, clients of the mental health services seek relationship based practice from their social workers. Here (Department of Health 2008) is the argument in relation to the Care Programme Approach:

> Services should be organised and delivered in ways that promote and co-ordinate helpful and purposeful mental health practice based on fulfilling therapeutic relationships and partnerships between the people involved. These relationships involve shared listening, communicating, understanding, clarification, and organisation of diverse opinion to deliver valued, appropriate, equitable and co-ordinated care. The quality of the relationship between service user and the care co-ordinator is one of the most important determinants of success.

Again, emphasis is placed on qualities such as listening and communicating, and such qualities only arise within the context of a relationship. And deep listening, and communication that goes beyond the superficial, will usually be present only where trust has developed through time and by constancy.

The level of client–worker engagement that is being described here goes not only to the depths of the client, but of the social worker also. That is, relational social work is both *inter*personal and *intra*personal. No social worker can listen in depth to their client and not engage themselves as a person, albeit a professional person. A social work student described this kind of relationship by saying that 'part of yourself is part of the practice', and her words encapsulate the personal involvement that relational social work requires of the worker. Who social workers are cannot meaningfully be separated from what they do, and this way of practising, its depths and its boundaries, will be important aspects of the book.

## THE SOCIAL WORK TASK FORCE

This emphasis on the personhood of the social worker is increasingly to be found in formal documents that set out directions for the future of social work. For example, the report from the Social Work Task Force (2009) argues that the process of selecting who will become a social work student should include 'opportunities to reflect on life experience', so that what is *intra*personal is explicitly seen as having an effect of what is *inter*personal. Students, the report argues, must have the 'right mix of intellectual and personal qualities' and, accordingly, this book will provide you with opportunities to assess and develop your personal qualities in ways that are consistent with social work theory, values and practice. The Social Work Task Force also stresses the importance of allowing adequate time for case analysis and supervision, seeing these as making possible 'the fine judgements at the heart of successful social work'. Again, this book will discuss these dimensions of social work practice and provide you with opportunities to relate them to yourself.

## SOME NOTES ON TERMINOLOGY

Throughout the book you will find a mixture of feminine and masculine pronouns used to describe social workers and their clients. Sometimes the gender matters. For example, one case study discusses the psychological impact on a social worker who hears she is to have a hysterectomy. At other times the gender is less important, or irrelevant – thus making it possible for the reader to substitute 'he' for 'she', or vice versa, without making any difference to the point under discussion.

A further question about terminology revolves round the use of 'client' or 'service user', or (as in some local authorities) 'customer'. My feeling about 'customer' is that it is language which derives from economically based market relations and, as such, is alien to the founding principles of the welfare state and social work – that is, the provision of a service which is universally available, and never based on the ability to 'buy' – a condition that the word 'customer' implies. But what of 'client' or 'service user'?

There is an element of subjective judgement at work here. Two social work authors (Thompson and Thompson 2008: xxiv) state it like this:

> There is no ideal term, but my preference is for 'client' as it is a term I associate with professionalism and a commitment to treating people with respect, rather than 'service user' which has connotations of a service-led mentality.

A similar sentiment, but giving additional reasons for the choice, may be found in a Community Care (2008) online discussion:

> Personally, I see the term 'service user' as mildly derogative. Maybe it's the word 'user', which has mostly negative connotations. I much prefer the term 'client', which I feel offers a certain amount of dignity to the person involved with the service. Connotations associated with this word are those of the person having some degree of choice and of working in partnership with the service.

It is possible to find protagonists to support either side of this debate. With reference to this book the word 'client' is used more often, although the term service user is adopted when illustrating the argument (in Chapter 7) that the social services worker is someone who is appointed to be in the *service* of their client. As with the use of 'he' or 'she', there is no reason why a reader, if they wish, should not mentally substitute 'service user' for 'client' as they read.

## THE STRUCTURE OF THE BOOK

The book is divided into eight chapters, some focusing on theory about relationships and others more on practice. In several chapters there are exercises that will help you to apply the theory or the practice to yourself and it is this emphasis on the *personal application* of ideas which lies at the heart of the book's teaching. And so, from the outset, you are encouraged to use the book for intellectual and cognitive learning but also for emotional and personal development. What is meant here will become clearer as you begin to work your way through the chapters but, in this introduction, it is important to emphasise this dual nature of the text. It is about social work theory and practice, but it is also about *you* and your development as a student social worker in relationship with yourself and with others.

Chapter 2 argues that relationships are of central importance to social work because they are of central importance to humanity. Any claim by social work that it is a human discipline must imply that human relating lies at its heart, and forms of doing social work that distance workers from their relationships with clients are distancing social work from its humanistic foundations. The chapter will discuss the importance of developing skills in relating not only to others but also to oneself. Thus, an ongoing theme of the book is introduced – that relationship based practice is both *inter*personal and *intra*personal.

Chapter 3 enters more deeply into the theoretical bases of relationship based social work. Here you will see the crucial part played by relationships in the bio-psycho-social development of a child, and how a child's self-identity is formed within a relational matrix. You will be given the opportunity to explore your own self-identity because relationship based social work requires you to enhance your awareness of the self that you will take with you into your professional practice.

Chapter 4 builds on the theoretical bases of Chapters 2 and 3 by providing you with further opportunities to develop relational skills by use of practical exercises in self-awareness. You will explore who you are, and locate yourself as a unique person within the more general dimensions of social work theory, practice and values. The chapter introduces the LIFELINE exercise which will be built upon in succeeding chapters.

Chapter 5 switches the focus from knowing yourself to knowing the other person. It emphasises the importance of both reason and emotion in assessing human situations, and introduces central ideas such as the theory and the practice of emotional intelligence and empathy. As in previous chapters, you will be provided with experiential opportunities that enable you to see where these ideas have fitted into relationships in your own life.

Chapter 6 focuses upon the demanding nature of relationship based social work and the requirement placed upon workers to sustain themselves by the use of reflection, mindfulness and professional supervision. Thus, looking after oneself is seen as a necessary condition for looking after one's clients but, more than this, appropriate self-care is a way of developing oneself and finding satisfaction in one's professional career.

Chapter 7 is concerned with the ethical bases of relational practice. The principle based approach to social work is discussed, but it is shown how relationship based practice requires this to be complemented by the ethics of care. This form of ethics is founded on the personalities of workers in relationship, their wanting to do what is 'best', and the relational capabilities that they can use to facilitate this end.

Chapter 8 concludes the book by locating the worker–client relationship within the greater context of human co-existence. And, by referring to the self-awareness work done throughout the book, it brings back into focus the personal life of the social worker, showing how even the most difficult experiences in a worker's life can be used positively in their relationship based practice.

# THE CENTRALITY OF RELATIONSHIPS IN SOCIAL WORK

**2**

## INTRODUCTION

This chapter begins to consider the central place that relationships take in the formation of the individual person. We are all affected profoundly by our experiences of relationships and this is why the relationship between a social worker and her client can alter the practice outcome. We shall consider some practical examples that illustrate this and, in doing so, show that the worker's relationship with *herself* is just as important as the one she has with her client. Finally, we shall start to examine the idea that it is through the worker–client relationship that a social worker can 'use herself' in a creative way.

## HUMAN RELATIONSHIPS AND WHY THEY MATTER

Human beings are interested in themselves. Throughout time they have developed increasingly sophisticated bodies of conceptual knowledge that help them to understand who and what they are. A core theme of this human quest for self-understanding has been that of relationships – a desire to explore the interpersonal connections that we form, borne out of the needs that we have for one another. These relational needs might be expressed at the most personal and private level with a lover, or as a comparatively impersonal transaction with a supermarket cashier. The word 'relationship' covers a large range of inter-human contact.

Relationships are a bit like the air we breathe. Though they are necessary for our existence – biological, social and psychological – we tend to take them for granted unless something exceptional happens. The exceptional might be falling in love, or falling out of love, or having an argument that makes us unhappy. In times like these relationships are on our mind, exercising a huge influence upon the way we feel.

It was the social and emotional effects of relationships that interested Argyle and Henderson (1985). They showed how a range of psychosocial indices were associated with either the creation of a new relationship or the loss of an existing one. For example, it is not surprising to learn that most people's mood is enhanced when they 'fall in love' but, by contrast, they found that the death rate for widowers rose by 40 per cent in the six months after their wife's death. Among the widowed and divorced there was an increased susceptibility to a range of physical disorders and, additionally, this group were more likely to become mentally ill, to become in-patients or commit suicide than were the married. Reinforcing the linkage between relationships and well-being, the authors cited a study which showed that people who were 'least connected' by marriage or friendships were likely to die earlier than those who were 'most connected'. And, in a later work, Argyle (1987) showed how the 'happiness' a person feels, their vulnerability to distress and ill health, their self-esteem, were all correlated to their intimacy (or lack of it) with others.

Human relationships, and usually their *quality* or their *loss*, form the ordinary content of everyday social work. In nearly all social work transactions relationships are involved somewhere and, in some instances such as bringing a child into care, the breakdown of a relationship is often at the heart of the matter.

## THEORISING ABOUT RELATIONSHIPS

The bodies of conceptual knowledge about human relationships that have been of most interest to social work are the psychological and the sociological, but, more recently, the discipline of neuroscience has become important too. Each of these disciplines is providing the profession of social work with valuable information about the effects that relationships have upon the individual person.

Psychologists ask radical questions about why individuals think and feel and behave in the ways that they do and of key interest to them have been questions about why we differ from one another (Ewen 1993), and why we are similar to one another. What kinds of influences, biological, psychological and social, combine to make an individual's *personality* (Ewen 1993, Maltby et al. 2007) and, when we try to analyse or 'make sense' of why we think, feel and act in certain ways, how much weight should we give to each influence? Different branches of psychology have arrived at different answers to these questions (Ingleby 2006).

In a similar way, sociologists and anthropologists have asked why societies are shaped in the ways that they are, what functions are served by social institutions and cultural patterns, and why societies differ from one another in the ways that they do things (Bilton et al. 2002). Most relevant and important from social work's point of view has been the way that sociologists have studied and conceptualised the social construction of the person – how individuals are moulded by the 'reality' of the societies into which they are born (Berger and Luckman 1991) and how their relational behaviours are determined largely by the expectations and norms that are present in social groups (Argyle 1968, Goffman 1990 [1959], Hogg and Vaughan 2005). A relevant example for social workers is that a behaviour which one society defines as 'abusive' could be regarded as normal and acceptable in another.

These kinds of psychological and sociological arguments have been complemented in more recent years by exciting developments in the field of neuroscience

(Schore 2001a and 2001b, Gerhardt 2004b). The evidence emerging here shows us how the individual human brain is psychosocially formed, how neural pathways are 'cut' at an early stage of our life, and how these pathways continue to influence our patterns of thinking and feeling and behaving throughout our lifetime.

The theoretical bases of these bio-psycho-social ideas will be discussed more fully in the next chapter. For the present the important idea for you to engage with is that some researchers in the discrete areas of psychology, sociology and neurology are converging in their ideas about how the individual is formed. Increasing attention is being given to the basic proposition that each person, with their unique pattern of thinking, feeling and behaving, is (to a greater or lesser extent) created within a matrix of human relationships. It is human contact that in large part constructs who and what we are as individual persons.

This convergence of ideas from otherwise separate areas of the human sciences is of critical importance to social work theory and practice.

## SOCIAL WORK PRACTICE: USING THEORY TO GUIDE WHAT WE DO

Throughout its history, the social work profession has been drawn towards those theories that help it to understand and work creatively with human relationships (Biestek 1961, Taft 1973, Seden 2005, Miller 2006, Howe 2009). Social workers have not only regarded relationships as the *method* and the *medium* through which they engage with their clients (Ferard and Hunnybun 1972 [1962], Perlman 1979), but they have also long understood that knowledge of their clients' relational patterns, the human 'systems' within which their clients interact (Bronfenbrenner 1979) and changing relational patterns over the lifespan (Crawford and Walker 2007), form core elements of social work assessment.

For example, as social workers whose specialism is families and children gain new awareness about what kinds of relational experiences the infant child needs if he is to thrive (Howe 1995, Schore 2001a and 2001b, Gerhardt 2004b), so assessments in areas such as emotional abuse will be able to pinpoint more accurately the kinds of relational behaviours that place a child at risk (Howe 1995).

Within adult care, social work practice in mental health will equally be informed by our expanding knowledge about human relations. For example, social workers whose practice lies with emotional trauma, the adult survivors of abuse, the depressed and anxious, will be able to understand more about how their clients' relational histories have affected their mental states.

## SOCIAL WORK PRACTICE: USING THEORY TO UNDERSTAND OURSELVES

It is logical that the spurt of growth in our knowledge about the influence of relationships on others also applies to *ourselves*. If social workers are learning that relationship experiences are so critical to their clients' social and emotional well-being, it becomes a requirement and responsibility of professional development that they should also consider their own relationships, and how they affect their lives and their work with their clients. Such a self-consideration is fundamental to reflective practice in social work (Harrison and Ruch 2007, Knott and Scragg 2007).

This idea of applying relationship knowledge and theory to oneself introduces a central theme of this book. That is, the professional *inter*-relationship that a social worker has with her client cannot be discussed meaningfully without reference to the *intra*-relationship the worker has with herself. Expressed at its most simple level, on any one day a worker's mood, her emotional state, the thoughts that preoccupy her, her level of self-esteem – all these things will have effects (even if only minor and subtle) on how she relates with her colleagues and clients. And her awareness and management of her moods, their causes, and their effects on other people is a mark of her emotional intelligence (Howe 2008).

This is why the National Occupational Standards (NOS) for Social Work require students to:

> Reflect on your own background, experiences and practice that may have an impact on the relationship (with the service user) (Performance Criteria for Key Role 1)

Aspects of this most important criterion for relationship practice will be discussed more thoroughly, with accompanying practical exercises, in Chapters 3–6 of this book. For now, it is sufficient to point out that social workers, like their clients, are bio-psycho-socially formed, and they will therefore have a personality that is marked by habitual ways of thinking, feeling and behaving in relationships. Basic questions such as, does the social worker suffer from anxiety or depression, or does she generally feel good about herself, become relevant because moods such as these will affect her relational practice. Her personality, her *inner world*, and her external, professional performance do not exist independently – each is affected by the other (Schofield 1998).

## THE PERSONAL AND THE PROFESSIONAL: USING THE SELF IN PROFESSIONAL PRACTICE

At this stage I will do nothing more than introduce another key theme of this book. If a worker's personality is so closely linked to her professional performance the question arises – how can she *use* her personality and her inner world of thoughts and feelings to best effect? In essence this is a question about using oneself within one's professional repertoire. In later chapters it will be seen that learning to bring into work one's thoughts and feelings, to use one's own experiences, when done appropriately, can benefit the client and be the basis for meeting the NOS requirements to

- enable people to express, explore and assess their feelings and emotions;
- sustain people through the process of change;
- develop a supportive relationship;

- build honest relationships based on clear communication;
- be good at starting, continuing and closing relationships.

So far, consideration has been given to ideas from psychology, sociology and neuroscience that suggest a person is formed through relationships, and the argument has been that these ideas are important to the social work profession because human relationships have always been at its heart. This relational centrality can be thought of in two ways – firstly, using the worker–client relationship as a method of engaging with the client and, secondly, understanding the client's relational framework (or absence of it) as a core element of assessment.

The reflective and emotionally intelligent practitioner will also apply these relational ideas to him or herself, and it is this self-application which will become the basis of *using* the self within one's professional practice.

Now, the use of some practical case examples will help to illustrate the theoretical ideas.

## CASE EXAMPLES AND REFLECTION QUESTIONS

In the following case examples you should consider three aspects of relationships in social work with their accompanying skills. These are:

1   Skills in relating to others.
2   Skills in relating to self.
3   Skills in relating to self and others.

## SKILLS IN RELATING TO OTHERS – THE *INTER*PERSONAL

What follows is a learning exercise that is designed to start you thinking about the crucial influence that the relationship between a social worker and client can have on the development of a case. I suggest that you read it slowly and meditatively, try to imagine yourself in the emotional position of the client, and pause to reflect on the questions after each stage.

 **Case Study One**

**Stage 1**

Nick is a client who suffers from chronic anxiety and agoraphobia. He lives alone in a one-bedroom flat that is rented from a housing association. His mental condition has been the cause of him stopping work. For more than a year he has been visited by the same social worker from the Community Mental Health Team (CMHT).

She has been working progressively with him to improve his self-confidence and whenever she has visited he finds that his level of anxiety is decreased. This has reached the stage where he makes bus journeys with her to the town, and she has made the suggestion that he might progress towards working for a few hours a week in a charity shop.

- Now, take some time to 'think' and 'feel yourself' into Nick's social and emotional position in relation to the social worker.
- What words come to mind to describe your thoughts and feelings?

**Stage 2**

One day the social worker visits, as usual. But the visit becomes unusual when gently she breaks the news to Nick that she has been successful in applying for a managerial position, and that another social worker from the CMHT will be taking her place.

- Take time to 'feel yourself' into Nick's new social and emotional position in relation to the social worker.
- What words come to mind to describe your feelings?

**Stage 3**

The day arrives when the social worker visits with the colleague who is to take over her role. After the introductions are made the new social worker asks Nick about his anxiety and agoraphobia. She seems to have a good understanding of these conditions, and she listens attentively and responds with empathy. But, despite this, for Nick it 'feels different'. When she asks him if he would like to continue making the bus journeys into town he is not quite sure. She senses his uncertainty, and suggests that it is discussed together next time she visits.

- Take time to 'feel yourself' into Nick's social and emotional position in relation to the new worker.
- What words come to mind to describe your feelings?

## What has altered?

In this exercise you have imagined yourself to be a client who has experienced two social workers. Both workers were sensitive, patient and understanding. Each had the practical skills of listening and empathic responding, and each had the theoretical understanding of anxiety and agoraphobia. Yet to the client it *felt different*.

Words may have sprung to mind as you tried to describe Nick's feelings about the change of worker. Possibly you came up with terms such as *insecure, uncertain* or *afraid*. It seems that Nick had placed his trust in the first worker and when the relationship changed, although the new worker displayed similar practical skills and theoretical knowledge, his trust gave way to uncertainty.

In order to understand why this change took place the situation must be looked at from a *relational* point of view. Doing this helps you to see that the trust and confidence existed *in the relationship* between the social worker and Nick, and *not* in the practical skills and theoretical knowledge that she brought (crucial though these are to trust-building). This illustrates the argument made by Seden (2005: 15) that 'it is the personal relationship and facilitating qualities of the worker that are valued, as much as the skills and theoretical models'. This is the key point to take from this case example. Some of this client's worst panic-inducing thoughts, such as being abandoned in the town, had subsided because, it seems, he trusted *who* the social worker was as a person at least as much as *what* she was as a professional with specialist knowledge.

Reflection questions

- In a situation like this, is there a reason to believe that the new social worker could, over time, gain Nick's trust?
- What qualities would the worker–client relationship require for trust to grow?

## A practice point to consider

Whenever a social worker takes a new client on to his or her caseload, it is good practice to reflect upon what the person may need in order to construct with them, where possible, a creative and co-operative relationship. The worker's initial reflections may change in the light of meeting the person but, nevertheless, this can be a valuable way of preparing the self for a first encounter.

This case referred to Nick who suffers from anxiety and agoraphobia. Knowing this in advance, and reflecting upon what might reduce Nick's relational anxieties, the new social worker could have concluded that she should practise in a way that is predictable, steady and reliable – challenging, but not demanding too much change too quickly.

The general practice point to learn from this is that in many circumstances social workers are able to prepare for their first encounter with a new client *before* the meeting takes place. Often, the way a client experiences a first meeting will affect subsequent encounters.

## SKILLS IN RELATING TO ONESELF – THE *INTRA*PERSONAL

Social workers sometimes focus on the skills of relating to others but neglect those of relating to themselves. Engaging in the process of knowing oneself (Trevithick 2005, Harrison and Ruch 2007, Koprowska 2008), of being intrapersonal, is a fundamental requirement of using relationships skilfully, and the following learning exercise is designed to help you to think about how self-knowledge relates to social work practice.

Read this account of social work practice stage by stage. Pause between each stage and give yourself time to engage with the points of reflection.

    Case Study Two

### Stage 1

Diana is a social worker with 10 years' experience in 'a looked-after children' team. For some years she has had on her caseload Jane, now 16 years old and living with foster parents, Dave and Geraldine. One day Geraldine phones to say that Jane is pregnant. Jane and Geraldine have been discussing whether or not she should have a pregnancy termination and they are requesting that Diana makes a visit to discuss the matter.

- Give thought to ways in which Diana could prepare herself mentally for this visit to Jane.

### Stage 2

Diana goes to the foster home as planned. The pregnancy is at an early stage. It is clear that Geraldine and Jane have a close relationship and, while sitting listening to them discussing the dilemma about whether or not to seek a termination, Diana has an unexpected feeling of discomfort and sadness come over her. The feelings grow in intensity to the point where she ceases to listen properly to what Geraldine and Jane are saying. Diana leaves at the earliest opportunity.

- What do we 'do' with unexpected emotions that arise during our work and occupy our minds?

### Stage 3

While driving home Diana dwells upon these unexpected feelings of discomfort and sadness. What has caused them? She reflects upon her own life and her own values. She has always felt uneasy about abortion, but has never said to herself or anyone else that she is *against* it. But now, her feelings of unease have become intense. She does not fully understand why this is so but she knows that the emotions, even if unspoken, could be sensed by Jane.

- Diana believes in the value of client self-determination. But in this case she is becoming aware that it could bring her into conflict with a deeply held personal value about the 'sanctity of life'. How should we handle emotions arising from our work that create a conflict within us?

### Stage 4

The next morning Diana feels no different and asks to see her manager. She explains to her how she feels, and her concerns that her emotions could influence her professional practice in such a way that Jane might find it difficult to make the right

*(Continued)*

*(Continued)*

decision for herself. Diana asks to be removed from the case. Her manager agrees to remove her from the case if that is her final decision, but asks her to consider first the effects this could have on Jane. How would it be explained to her, and would it make her feel guilty if she did have an abortion? The manager suggests another course in which Diana stays as the social worker and receives regular, supportive supervision. Diana is left to consider the options that she has.

- Think about what 'supportive supervision' would be for Diana. How would she use it, and what would the role of the superviser be?

Some of the learning points to draw from this case are that Diana recognised that her feelings could affect her client. Her questions to herself were, why am I feeling like this? How will my feelings affect my work? In asking these questions she increased her self-awareness, she became able to name what her feeling of discomfort was connected with, and she discussed it with her manager. In this way she maintained a truthful and constructive relationship, intrapersonally with herself, interpersonally with her client and professionally with her team.

## Points to consider on your own, or debate with others

- Is Diana the right social worker to enable Jane to express, explore and assess her feelings and emotions (adapted from NOS (National Occupational Standards for Social Work) Unit 5. Element 5.1)?
- Is Diana the right social worker to sustain Jane through a process of change (NOS, ibid.)?
- Could Diana continue to 'build honest relationships based on clear communication' (NOS, ibid.) with Jane, while remaining true to her own values?
- Could Diana maintain a supportive relationship if Jane decided on a pregnancy termination (NOS Unit 5. Element 5.1)?

## Personal feelings and professional practice

An argument is sometimes made that being professional means, in part, separating the self from personal feelings and carrying out the task in hand. This, so the argument would run, is the duty that a professional has to his or her client. But different professions are different. The social worker provides an interpersonal service and in this way she differs from, say, a structural engineer who is a professional working with concrete and steel.

Because social work is a personal service, both the client's and the social worker's thoughts and feelings matter (parallel arguments are made in other professions – see for example Zalidis 2001, Cocksedge 2005). Sometimes, and often in a mental health setting, it is the client's thoughts and feelings that are actually the focus of the social work involvement. And so we should see social work as a distinctive profession where separating oneself from one's emotions is tantamount to separating oneself from the client. Of course, this is *not* the same as saying that social work is an emotionally driven occupation. Rather, the emotionally intelligent (Howe 2008) social worker will be in touch with his or her feelings but be able to *manage* or *contain* them in such a way that the task at hand can be completed in a professional manner.

## Reflection points

Social workers come into close contact with human suffering and sadness. To withstand this an element of objectivity, robustness and resilience is required. But social workers also have the task of engaging sensitively with their client's feelings while, at the same time, managing their own emotional state in a way that is constructive, both for themselves and their client. A later chapter will consider this balance in more depth but for now it is sufficient to summarise the process of emotional management for professional practice. It involves activities and self-questioning:

- Bringing one's feelings to the level of full awareness and assessing, with the help of personal reflection, mindfulness and professional supervision (all topics for Chapter 6), how they affect the case.
- Asking, would my feelings adversely affect the client if they were known? Would they put undue pressure on a vulnerable client?
- Asking, would my feelings cause me to become over-subjective, and lose the necessary objectivity for social work assessment and judgement?
- Asking, can I use my emotions in my work in such a way that they become a constructive source for my client?

These questions recur throughout relationship based social work and in future chapters you will find them discussed in more detail.

## SKILLS IN RELATING TO SELF AND OTHERS – THE *INTRA*PERSONAL AND *INTER*PERSONAL COMBINED

The development of professional relationship skills requires learning to relate to, and explore the connections between, both your own inner world and that of your client.

Consider the following case study in which Louise, the social worker, unexpectedly experiences her innermost feelings as being in powerful resonance with those of her client, Rakhi. At times this resonance is so strong that she believes her feelings are the *same* as those being experienced by her client.

---

 **Case Study Three**

**Louise's personal circumstances**

Louise is a 35-year-old social worker. Her mind is much preoccupied by the recent medical advice she has received that she should undergo a hysterectomy. As this news sinks in she dwells upon what it means for her, for her partner, and for their hopes of having children.

**Louise's professional work**

Louise works in a community mental health team and one of her clients, Rakhi, is the mother of two children, Anshula and Sarvesh. Coinciding with Louise's news about the hysterectomy, Rakhi's children are received into voluntary care because her chronic mental disorder renders her temporarily unable to care for them.

At the level of emotion Louise and Rakhi may share similar and powerful feelings of profound loss, pervading hopelessness and depression. Louise is experiencing her own inner world in an intense way, and her engagement with Rakhi may further intensify this experience – as well as give her insight into what Rakhi is feeling.

**Reflection questions (individually or in small groups)**

Give some thought to the following questions:

- Under what circumstances could Louise and Rakhi having similar feelings be advantageous and creative for social work practice?
- Under what circumstances could the similarity of feelings be disadvantageous, or even damaging for social work practice?
- Should Louise tell Rakhi about her own sense of loss and feeling of depression?

The case of Louise and her client, Rakhi, describes a complex emotional situation that raises some fundamental questions about relationship based practice. Below there are some general points and answers to the questions, although you should bear in mind that each social worker/client relationship is unique – so there can be exceptions to the general rule.

**Learning points to take from the case study**

- Looked at objectively, Louise's role is not changed by her pending hysterectomy. She has the same duty to act towards Rakhi in ways that are helpful and therapeutic, in accordance with the Care Programme Approach. Louise should be sensitive to the breakdown in Rakhi's family life and alert to any risk factors that result from it.

- But Louise's intrapersonal world has changed. Her professional duty is to strive to be aware of her feelings and how they could affect her relationships and her work. She may clarify her feelings by talking with a colleague or through personal reflection or professional supervision.
- If Louise does this, she may decide to continue to work with Rakhi. In such circumstances her intrapersonal world could enhance the empathy that she feels for Rakhi, thereby deepening the interpersonal relationship between them. In this situation Louise is *using herself* as a resource for her work.
- This use of self does *not* mean that Louise should tell Rakhi about herself and her forthcoming hysterectomy. Relationship based practice should never be mistaken for friendship where an exchange of personal information is normal. So, while the worker–client relationship may be friendly, it always remains a *professional* relationship. Crossing the boundary into friendship can lead to over-involvement in clients' lives, and a worker divulging personal information, especially of a problematical kind, may cause clients to feel that they should not burden their social worker with their own problems. In Chapter 5 there is a fuller discussion of empathy and how it differs from sympathy. And in Chapter 8 there are further comments about workers' self-disclosures to their clients.

## MOVING TOWARDS A DEFINITION OF RELATIONSHIP BASED PRACTICE

Social work belongs with the group of professional services that can be described as 'personal'. One reason why it should be thought of in this way is that each time a social worker interacts with her clients her 'personality' – her unique combinations of thinking, feeling and behaving – comes into play. This personality, that can be thought of as 'who' she is (rather than 'what' she is as a social worker), is not a neutral factor with regard to her professional delivery. Rather, as seen in the case studies, who she is as a person is likely to affect, for better or for worse, the process and, possibly, the outcome of her professional engagements. In this sense social work is an activity in which the worker's personality is the conduit through which the professional delivery of services flows. The social worker's personhood can have a profound effect on her professionhood.

In social work the presence of the personal within the professional is inevitable. Social workers cannot help but take 'themselves' to their work as communicators, listeners, negotiators and supporters (Beckett 2006), and each 'self' will be unique to that social worker. Clients feel this, which is perhaps why they sometimes talk of 'my' rather than 'the' social worker. They can develop a proprietorial sense about the worker with whom they are engaged and, in this way, social work is not only a personal but also a personalising service, a relationship with others that can touch in intimate ways upon the most serious of life events and the deepest of human emotions.

There is mounting evidence that the relationships that social workers have with their clients hold the potential for creating radical changes in clients' perceptions of themselves and their environment (see, for example, Gilbert 2007). Constructing worker–client relationships that bring these benefits is not straightforward and, throughout this book, chapters will explore the skills, attitudes and values that go together to create relational practice. But for now, and in the most general sense, we can say that relationship based practitioners are workers who are sensitive to all that is relational between themselves and their client but, instead of letting this remain implicit, they seek appropriate ways of bringing the relationship to the fore-ground of their work. Their question is, now, in this professional encounter, how can I use and offer who I am in such a way that my personality or character becomes a resource that is creative and available to my client?

## Use of self – questions to ponder

- With an anxious client: how can I be with her in such a way that I help her to feel secure?
- With a mentally ill client: how can I be with him in such a way that I help him to feel accepted?
- With an abused client: how can I be with her in such a way that I help her to feel safe?

In effect, and at a level which is judged appropriate, relationship based practition-ers place their own being in the service of their client – a kind of disposal of the self for the well-being of the other. These workers thereby elevate the inevitable exist-ence of the self-in-work into a conscious, organised, purposeful, ethical and, ideally, therapeutic tool that can be used within their interpersonal engagements. Their way of working tends towards merging their personality with their professional life so that, expressed ideally, a 'holistic' approach to work is achieved.

Certain conditions contribute towards the construction of creative relational practice and throughout the book we shall return to them, and to the acquisition of the skills that are required to practise social work in this kind of way. At this point all I will do is summarise what will be discussed in more detail in further chapters.

## A SUMMARY OF SOME RELATIONSHIP BASED PRACTICE SKILLS

- A commitment and growing ability to know the self (Howe 1993, Lishman 2002, Thompson 2005, Trevithick 2005).
- A commitment to try to know the other person – their life's influences, their ways of thinking and feeling and behaving.
- Purposefully raising these knowledges about self and other to consciousness – thinking and reflecting on them (Knott and Scragg 2007, Wilson et al. 2008).
- Using this conscious awareness where possible and appropriate to relate in deeper ways with the client, for the benefit of the client.
- Offering and using the self in the relationship.

Sometimes social work intervention is short term and the focus is prescribed tightly by the agency's core task. In such a setting it may not be possible to work fully in a relational manner. At others times and, in particular, in long term work with children and families or mental health teams, a relational engagement becomes not only possible but also desirable. Often, in these areas of social work, it is insecure and abusive relationships that have brought clients to the social work service. In such circumstances relationship based practice can become a kind of relational remedy – using the same medium of the human relationship but in ways that are constructive rather than destructive, growthful and life enhancing rather than stunting.

## SUMMARY

- People's social and emotional states are closely linked with their relationship experiences. People are changed by relationships.
- What is true for clients is also true for social workers. That is, their interpersonal and intrapersonal relationships have a huge effect on their thoughts, feelings and behaviours.
- Social workers' relationships with themselves will affect their relationships with their clients.
- Relationships are the medium through which social work conducts its business. The skilled social worker will be able to relate in creative ways both to herself and to others. She will be accomplished at *using* herself in relationships.
- The worker's use of herself will be the basis on which she will meet some important NOS.

 *Further reading*

Allan, Clare 'My brilliant survival guide', *Guardian*, 14 January 2009 – accessed through http://www.guardian.co.uk/society/2009/jan/14/mental-health-clare-allan-social-worker.
This article provides a client's view about how important the relationship with her social worker was to her recovery.

Ruch, G., Turney, D., Ward, A. (2010) *Relationship Based Social Work: getting to the heart of practice*. London and Philadelphia: Jessica Kingsley Publications.
This collection of essays discusses the context and the theory of relationship based social work and the use of self.

Wilson, K., Ruch, G., Lymbery, M., Cooper, A. (2008) *Social Work: an introduction to contemporary practice*. Harlow, Pearson Education.
This is a general book about the theory and practice of social work which places emphasis on the client–worker relationship.

Winter, K. (2011) *Building Relationships and Communicating with Young Children*. London and New York: Routledge.
This book sets out in powerful manner how children have sometimes been failed by the quality of social work relationships, and how relational methods are at the heart of communicating with children.

# 3    THE THEORETICAL BASES OF RELATIONSHIP BASED SOCIAL WORK

## INTRODUCTION

Chapter 2 focused on the fact that relationships matter very much to human beings, and that social work practice outcomes are altered by the relationship that a worker has, both with herself and with her client.

This chapter will delve deeper into these topics by exploring *psychosocial science* and *neuroscience*. From different evidence bases these disciplines have arrived independently at the common and central tenet – that our experiences of relationships with other people, and especially our early attachments, have major effects upon our lives. In particular, evidence will be examined which suggests that the qualitative aspects of our relationships play a large part in our moods throughout our lifespan – explaining our happiness or our discontent. Relationships can underpin chronic and acute depression and anxiety disorders. They can help us to build up a strong sense of personal identity, or leave us feeling fractured and uncertain about our roles in life. Hence our relationships with others are a huge influence upon our relationship with our *self*, our self-image and self-esteem. We come to experience and know who we are by the way others treat us.

In exploring the disciplines of psychosocial science and neuroscience the chapter will provide you with foundational knowledge about the formation of the person. It will equip you to answer the question of *why* relationships matter so much to social work and it will map on to the knowledge base for NOS Key Role 1. In particular this Key Role requires you to be conversant with psychological and sociological explanations of:

- human growth and development and the factors that impact upon it;
- mental health and well-being;
- social interactions and relationships;
- human behaviour;
- theories and methods of promoting personal, social and emotional well-being.

By reading the chapter you should obtain a basic knowledge of contemporary thinking about the ways in which a developing child is formed by relationships, and how this formation affects his or her adult life.

You are also asked to complete three class exercises that will help you to apply the ideas to a case study and to aspects of your own life.

The chapter acts as a prelude to Chapter 4 where the focus is upon the importance of relationships in social work practice and how to prepare oneself for this professional way of being.

## BECOMING RELATIONAL: THE PSYCHOSOCIAL CONSTRUCTION OF THE RELATIONAL SELF

Although sociology and psychology are separate disciplines, within the area of human development they have converged to the point where they are regarded as two sides of the same coin. That is, our 'inner' world which is the focus of psychology affects, and is affected by, our 'outer' world which is the focus of sociology. And there is one concept in particular that has attracted the attention of both psychologists and sociologists because it spans both inner and outer worlds. It is the concept of the *self*.

It is no exaggeration to say that for some branches of psychology the 20th century was the century of the self. For example, a major preoccupation for psychologists has been the exploration of the processes whereby the infant child *becomes* or *constructs* their self (Fonagy et al. 2002), and how they continue to *maintain* and *develop* this sense of 'who I am' throughout the lifespan (Boyd and Bee 2008). The evidence that has emerged consistently suggests that this self develops in relationships with others, and the nature of these relationships – positive and life-enhancing or negative and stultifying – will affect the psychosocial trajectory that life takes. In order to illustrate this, psychologists have developed a number of concepts, many of which have found their way into everyday language.

The 20th century starting point for the psychology of the self is Freud (1971 [1900]) and the notion that the self (or 'ego') is a fragile construction that must be *defended* from the biological, psychological and sociological tensions that are intrinsic to humanity. For example, a married mother might be sexually drawn towards a man with whom she works. The physical attraction is compelling. But in her mind she feels profound guilt and disloyalty to her husband. Freud's interest was in how such a woman, in such an everyday type of human situation, maintains her psychological and social stability. His answer was that human beings develop and employ *defence mechanisms* that, to an extent, protect the self from internal tension, from fears and anxieties and, perhaps, from complete psychological disintegration. Among these defence mechanisms are *denial* about what is happening, a conscious mental act of thought suppression. Another method of defence is *repression,* pushing the guilt-inducing wishes into the unconscious mind, thus making them less troubling and disruptive to everyday life. A further way of psychologically managing what threatens to disintegrate the integrity of the self is by this woman *projecting* her own inner world of thoughts and feelings onto another woman. Thus it becomes the other woman and not she who desires this man. And yet another projective defence would be to convince herself that it is the man who desires her, thereby putting herself in the controlling position of rejecting his imagined and 'unwelcome' advances.

The case illustrates an essential aspect of Freud's understanding of the self: that is, it requires protection *from itself*, such is the power of the inner conflicts which arise from tension between primary instincts and living in a 'civilised' society where instinctual impulses are regulated by social conventions. Freud's thinking began what has become an ongoing process of enquiring what the self is, what kinds of life experiences affect self-development and, in particular, affect the self's ability to remain intact and stable amidst the inherently unstable conditions of human existence.

The large amount of attention that psychologists have given to the concept of the self has been mirrored, though not on quite the same scale, by sociologists. For example, Goffman's (1990 [1959]) interest was in how the self *interacts* with and *presents* itself in its encounters with others. He saw individual selves as engaged in a drama, each playing *roles*. Thus, selves are *performances* that are acted out in such a way that the *impression* that the self makes on others is *managed* by the actor. Goffman was also interested in situations where role performances or *identities* are *spoiled* (for example, when unexpected or embarrassing things happen), or individuals are *stigmatised,* and the effects this has on both the subject and the other participants in the drama. Similar thinking may be seen in the work of micro-sociologists such as Garfinkel (1967) who concentrated upon how selves give meaning to experiences, how meanings are shared by social groups who construct behavioural and perceptual norms, and how these are mirrored back to reinforce the self of individual actors.

From the work of theorists such as Freud and Goffman it can be seen that the concept of the self has been shared by psychology and sociology, and often the two disciplines are attempting to explain the same phenomenon from their different perspectives. The central idea is that a person's inner world, their experience of *their* self, is largely influenced by their outer experiences and, in particular, their relational experiences. We are shaped by others, by the opinion we believe others have of us, by the opinion that we want to have of ourselves, and how these opinions are represented in our minds (Fonagy et al. 2002). What follows is a selection of work from a range of theorists that will help you to build up a picture of how the relational self is formed by relational experiences. You will see that the self is, to a great extent, a creation of others.

## CONSTRUCTING THE SELF – THE PIONEERING WORK OF COOLEY AND MEAD

A contemporary view of social psychology claims that 'Selves are constructed, modified and played out in interaction with other people' (Hogg and Vaughan 2005: 139). This perspective builds on the pioneer work of social psychologists such as Charles Horton Cooley (1902) and George Herbert Mead (1934).

For Cooley, part of the growth of the relational self consists in the development of an understanding about other people's minds. It is through our interactions with others that we learn to have their minds, their thoughts and feelings, *within our own mind*. This interconnection between self and others is summed up in his 'looking glass' analogy. Here, a person can think about their reflection in the mirror in three ways that together construct a 'self-idea'. They are

> the imagination of our appearance to the other person; the imagination of his judgement of that appearance, and some sort of self-feeling, such as pride or mortification. (Cooley 1902, in Manis and Meltzer 1967: 217)

Here, Cooley is beginning to analyse a person's construction of the emotional self based upon what he or she believes other people's opinions to be. It is what he calls an 'imputed sentiment, the imagined effect of this reflection upon another's mind' (Cooley 1902, in Manis and Meltzer 1967: 217). In a child this kind of emotional construction can lead to the first experiences of pride or shame, of guilt, worthiness or unworthiness. What a child believes people believe about him can become a reality in the child's mind. And, as will be shown later, such primary feelings and self-conceptions, constructed through relationships that are imagined or real, can have critical effects on the individual person's subsequent emotional state and health.

The work of Mead (1934) reinforces that of Cooley. He understands the development of the self in relationship as a process of action and reaction – of interaction between self and others. His conceptual framework used the idea of 'I' to describe the individual who has yet to be formed by his relational environment, and the idea of 'Me' as one who is increasingly adapting his 'I' to take account of relational influences.

Again, it can be seen that other people metaphorically *live* in our brain and a person develops a 'Me' 'in so far as he can take the attitude of another and act toward himself as others act ... hence the origin and foundations of the self ... are social' (Mead 1934: 171–173). In Mead's model we might wonder what others think about us, whether they love us, approve of us, dislike us or think we are boring – and we may adapt our behaviour to take account of our wondering.

In their work both Cooley and Mead were beginning to study systematically how the human mind, created by relational experiences, builds up habitual ways of thinking and feeling about the self and other people. It is this cognitive and emotional construction that forms the basis of personal *identity* – a concept that became hugely influential in our understanding of the self.

## PERSONAL IDENTITY: THE WORK OF ERIKSON

Building upon but adding a more social dimension to the Freudian ideas that first influenced him, Erik Erikson (1995 [1950]) was interested in how a human being forms a sense of self, the *ego*, and then preserves and develops this sense across the lifespan. A key concept was that of personal *identity* which he thought of as having four aspects.

1   *Individuality* – the person's sense of uniqueness, distinctness, separateness.
2   *Wholeness, indivisibility and synthesis* – the bringing together or synthesising of fragmentary parts of the self into a whole. This is a special task for the child and adolescent, but it continues over the lifespan.
3   *Sameness and continuity* – striving for a sense of inner sameness and continuity between who one has been in the past and who one is likely to be in the future. A feeling that one's life is going in a meaningful direction.
4   *Social solidarity* – a sense of inner solidarity with the ideals and values of a group which provides social support and validation. The individual's identity (constructed by 1–3 above) becomes meaningful and recognisable to others with whom he relates (adapted from Ewen 1993: 240).

These four aspects, if realised, represent a psychosocial life position in which the individual has successfully developed and sustained a settled sense of the self and its relationships with others in the social world. For Erikson, *identity* provides the foundation from which we relate to ourselves and others. It is a platform for our self-projection. It is our explanation and our experience of who we are and, through it, we are enabled to extend ourselves outwards into the relational world of others. Obtaining, sustaining and developing our personal identity is a lifelong process.

When things go wrong with our identity formation we are likely to experience what he called *identity confusion*. We feel unclear about 'who' we are and may relate to others in ways that confuse them. If this identity confusion is not satisfactorily resolved it will leave a person with feelings of inner disintegration and external uncertainty about his or her relationships and life's direction.

 **Case Study One**

**A confusion of identity**

John is aged 24 and married to Helen. They have two children aged two and three.

John and Helen have known one another since they were at school together 10 years ago. In his teenage years John experienced heterosexual feelings and he became Helen's sexual partner. But he was also attracted towards young men. As his relationship with Helen deepened and their families moved towards the expectation that one day they would marry, he told Helen about his uncertain sexual orientation. Together they decided that it was something that would 'pass' after they were married.

Now John has fallen in love with another man. He is experiencing a range of feelings – confusion, anger, guilt, entrapment – and he is profoundly unhappy and unsure about where his life is heading. He has withdrawn himself sexually from Helen. She has guessed what the problem is.

In terms of Erikson's theory about personal development John is experiencing a confused identity. Relating this view to the case study, and looking back at the four aspects of identity, we see that his life position has within it what appear to be fragmentary and irreconcilable elements:

1   His true sense of 'who' he is sexually is felt strongly and he is striving towards his individuality and uniqueness.

2   But this striving brings with it the experience of fragmentation and the inability to synthesise it with his status as a husband and father.

3   He is contemplating a radical personal change and the comforts of sameness and continuity that help to form identity are weakened within him.

4   He feels unsure about whether he can count on the social support and validation from family and friends that his identity partly depends upon. His relationship with himself and relationships with his closest others are in flux.

The case study illustrates the ways in which identity, how we experience ourselves inwardly as integrated or disintegrated, has a critical influence upon the ways in which we project ourselves outwardly into the world of social relationships. The intrapersonal and the interpersonal are inextricably linked.

The following exercise will help you to develop your skill in discerning feelings and in seeing how, when feelings conflict with one another, they may disturb a person's identity. Such a person finds it more difficult to know 'who' they are, they may lose confidence in the 'self' and, as a consequence, their relationships with others can become confused and confusing.

---

   **Practical work based on Case Study One**

**Discerning feelings (Done individually or in a small group)**

1   Imagine what John is feeling. Put into single words (e.g. frustrated, sad, helpless, excited, anxious, free, afraid…) the feelings that come into your mind.

2   Note in particular feelings that are in tension with one another – for example 'free' and 'trapped'.

3   Do the same for Helen. In what ways might she be experiencing identity confusion? What might she be feeling?

4   How do these feelings affect the personal identities of John and Helen?

5   How might these changes in personal identity begin to affect their relationships with one another?

---

General learning points to take from the case study and exercise are that many people become clients of social workers because their personal identities have not been adequately formed, or have come under assault from social and psychological traumas. This may be true of clients who have had neglectful or abusive childhoods, who are in care, or who have been brought up in care. Equally, adults who seek help from mental health practitioners may be experiencing a fractured self-identity with accompanying symptoms of social anxiety and depression. Personal identity is needed for a sense of integration, but everyday life experiences can threaten its disintegration. The exercise helps you to access the inner emotional worlds of John and Helen, exploring them empathically because empathic worker–client relationships lie at the heart of relational social work (see Chapter 6).

Erikson emphasised that the task of seeking an integrated identity was lifelong. He described it as our '*inner* population of remembered and anticipated sensations and images' interacting with our '*outer* population of familiar and predictable things and people' (Erikson 1995 [1950]: 222, emphasis added). Identity is strong when the 'outer population' act in accordance with inner anticipation. Conversely, it is weak, perhaps to the point of disintegration, when inner and outer are in tension or conflict. Each person is involved in a never ending process of managing as creatively as they may the 'vicissitudes' of their sexuality, the aptitudes that they are born with, and the opportunities offered by their societies and social roles. Erikson was an important analyst in what became known as 'ego psychology' and his lasting influence can be seen in the work of later theorists such as Heinz Kohut (1984).

The following exercise provides you with the opportunity to explore *your* personal identity. It asks you 'who' you are, and what identity you project into your relationships with others. You will also listen to another person's identity and attempt to empathise by trying to put into words the way your exercise partner might have felt about parts of his or her life.

---

**Exercise One**

**Who are you? (Done individually and in pairs)**

There has been a considerable amount of research on children's self-identities and the ways in which these take on typical characteristics of surface or depth at different ages (see Part 5 of Bee and Boyd, 2007). As children get older they normally increase their ability to dig below the surface of their lives by exploring their feelings and innermost ideas.

Social workers who want to practise relationally have a particular responsibility (see Chapter 4) to become more aware of the effects that their life experiences and relationships have had upon them. This exercise helps you to enhance your self-awareness.

Below is a brief and descriptive account of self-identity from an imaginary male social work student. You can use it as a suggested pattern for the personal exercise that follows it.

**Adam's self-identity**

My name is Adam. I am Anglo-Indian and 20 years old. Until I started university last year I lived with my mother and my sister who is 16. My dad has married again and he has two more children aged seven and nine. I haven't seen my dad since I was seven years old, but last year he wrote to me and asked me to make contact. I have not replied yet. I am pleased that he got in touch, but I don't know what to say to him. My mother is a schoolteacher. I am very close to her and to my sister, and I text them most days. I have girl friends but no one special. I'm friendly, but find women easier to get on with than men. I'm a runner, training for my first marathon. Running helps me with my studies. I really want to do social work. Partly I got on to the course because I'd been volunteering with older people. I'm looking forward to my social work placements.

## Part 1

### Describing and analysing your self-identity

- Spend a few minutes thinking about your own self-identity and, when you have some ideas describe them in a sentence form, as in the example above, or use bullet points.
- Now, try to go beyond description and ask yourself *why* you are as you are. Think about Freud and defending the self from impulsive drives, about Cooley and Mead and developing a 'me' that (to some extent) is devised to be acceptable to others, and Erikson's ideas that the maintenance of authentic self-identity might bring with it psychological and social conflict.
- What influences (both positive and negative) have relationships with family and friends had in creating your self-identity?

## Part 2

### Telling another person about yourself and practising empathy

This practical exercise is done in pairs – one speaker and one listener.

The listener should try to listen intently, without interrupting the speaker. Try to observe any 'body language' that the speaker displays as they describe aspects of 'who they are'.

For the speaker, the exercise gets you more used to telling another person about yourself and, as you do so, you may increase your self-awareness by clarifying what you feel about aspects of your life.

The exercise is in two stages:

1 Talk with your partner about your self-identity notes (divulging only as much about yourself as you feel comfortable with). Tell your partner about yourself and the influences that have made you who you are.
2 When you have finished it is your partner's task to try to empathise with aspects of your life. This is done in a simple way by *suggesting* what they think you might have felt like at different times in your life. They might say something like 'I wonder if you felt relieved when...'

When the two parts of the exercise are completed swap roles so that the listener talks about their self-identity.

*(Continued)*

*(Continued)*

**Learning from Exercise One**

It is difficult to say how these exercises will work out because everyone will have their unique answer. But it is likely that you will have found it difficult to say 'who' you are, to express your 'inner self', without relating this self to either a person or a status (both external realities): e.g. 'I am Sarah's sister', 'I am a student', 'I am Muslim'...

Often we define ourselves in terms of the relationships that we have with other people and things. This helps us to learn that we are essentially relational beings and that our inner worlds are experienced by us as contingent upon outer worlds.

The exercises also help you to learn about your *self*, which is your most important tool for relationship based social work (and the primary focus for the next chapter). I hope that you have come to appreciate in a deeper way than before that 'you' are a psychosocial construction that has been built by others.

You were also given an opportunity to relate to another person in an emotionally intelligent way (an idea and practice to be explored in Chapter 5).

## KAREN HORNEY: PSYCHODYNAMIC-HUMANISTIC PSYCHOLOGY

Like Erikson, Karen Horney (1991 [1950]) bridged the gap between psychodynamic (more solitarily psychological) and humanistic (more social) models of human development. Her interest lay in how the 'neurotic' adult constructs strategies for relating to others as a result of his or her adverse relational experiences in childhood. These strategies, although functional during childhood in terms of bringing some comfort or release from fear, later become dysfunctional insofar as they are an obstacle to the person's healthy development and what she called 'self-realisation' in adulthood.

The kinds of adverse childhood experiences that Horney has in mind are relationships with parents or carers who are

> too wrapped up in their own neuroses to be able to love the child...In simple words they may be dominating, overprotective, intimidating, irritable...partial to other siblings, hypocritical, indifferent ...As a result the child does not develop a feeling of belonging, of 'we', but instead a profound insecurity... [or]...*basic anxiety*. (1991 [1950]: 18)

In Horney's model the child with basic anxiety experiences other people as 'hostile', and she identifies three ways in which the child can manage himself in this threatening environment:

> ... he may try to cling to the most powerful person around him; he may try to rebel and fight; he may try to shut others out of his inner life and withdraw emotionally from them. In principle, this means that he can move *toward*, *against*, or *away* from others. (1991 [1950]: 19 my emphasis)

These three psychosocial movements – that is, shifts in the brain and in the behaviour adopted by the child – become lasting strategies for managing the threats posed by relationships. The person who experiences relational anxiety may tend to move *towards* others by becoming compliant or unassertive, or *against* others by being aggressive or contrary, or *away* from others by becoming avoidant or introvert. Each one of these moves is a relational strategy for easing the anxiety that is felt. As Horney says, 'It does not matter what [the child] feels, if only he is safe' (1991 [1950]: 21).

The child or young person who is developing in these kinds of ways has little opportunity or emotional energy left to develop what humanistic psychologists call the 'true' or 'authentic self'. The young person is likely to adopt different strategies for emotional survival with different people; thus, Horney suggests, false identities are adopted, perhaps grandiose and narcissistic, or humble and self-deprecating. She likens this process to a cocker spaniel becoming a red setter – the living out of inauthentic images instead of one's true self.

Horney's work provides another example of the theme of this chapter: that is, human beings are formed and sometimes malformed by their relationships. The work of Cooley, Mead, Erikson and Horney has in common the principal idea that *who we are is a construction of how others have related to us.* We are made in relationship. Further evidence and ideas that add to this theme come from the perspective of Abraham Maslow.

## ABRAHAM MASLOW AND HUMANISTIC PSYCHOLOGY

Maslow's core interest was in how human beings could become their 'true selves'. He wanted to understand what the conditions were in which authentic personal development could take place and, like the theorists already considered, he argued that healthy (or unhealthy) development takes place in relationships.

Unlike Freud, Maslow had a hopeful view of human beings, believing that in their depths they are 'good, or beautiful or desirable' (1968: 196). Given this optimism about the human condition, he devoted much of his working life to an attempt to understand why people are often unhappy and destructive, both with themselves and with others. His conclusion was a variation on the relationally based arguments of Erikson, Horney and others. That is, some growing children meet with 'parental and cultural disapprovals' and they come under pressure to repress their 'urge to grow' (1968: 192–193) in ways that are naturally creative and pro-social. Their relational experiences diminish their opportunities to 'self-actualise' their authentic, constructive and loving self-identity.

The underlying analysis that Maslow provides to support his views is based upon what he understands as *instinctive* human needs that begin in childhood and follow through the life cycle. He divides these needs into two categories – 'D' or Deficiency needs, and 'B' or Being needs.

All growing children have Deficiency needs. For example, if they were not cared for they would be deficient in food, warmth, clothing, safety, and so on. They relate to others (their carers) in a self-centred manner, looking upon them as ones who can gratify their deficiencies, supply them with what they require, and protect them from danger.

But for Maslow the child instinctively needs more than food and shelter – she needs love and, if denied it, becomes 'love hungry', experiencing 'a deficiency disease, like salt hunger or the avitaminoses' (1968: 42). At first this love need is necessarily one of deficiency, a purely self-centred taking from the carer. But if the carer provides for the child at this developmental stage, then the Deficiency type of love gives way to love based upon Being needs. Positive emotional development takes place. A love evolves in which the child begins to take into account the being of the other person, the carer. The relationship between them becomes more reciprocal, rewarding and life-enhancing for both the giver and the receiver.

It is this Being kind of love, and its growth and development through the life course, that lies at the heart of Maslow's hopefulness for people. It is through Being love that we create one another as healthy persons. He writes that

> B love in a profound … sense creates the partner. It gives him a self-image, it gives him self-acceptance, a feeling of love-worthiness, all of which permit him to grow. It is a real question whether the full development of the human being is possible without it. (1968: 43)

Thus, Maslow's is a theory which, again, gives central position to the construction of the person in relationship. But Maslow was well aware that relationships can also be destructive and leave a child with nothing but Deficiency needs to take into adulthood. Parents whose lives are dominated by meeting their 'D' needs are unable to give themselves to the child in ways that develop the child's sense of being loved and becoming loving. Such a child has not experienced a human environment in which it can grow in accordance with its instinctive self for, unlike animals whose instincts play a determining part in their behaviour, human instincts are 'weak, subtle and delicate, very easily drowned out' by human society (1968: 190). This child, Maslow argues, will become frustrated and may experience dominating emotions (such as sadness or anger) that will affect all future relationships.

There follows a case study and, as you work your way through it, think about the development theories of Erikson, Horney and Maslow, and apply them to Matthew's life and psychosocial state.

---

   **Case Study Two**

**Applying theory to practice**

- **Matthew A (subject of case study) – aged 40 years**
- **Claire A (deceased) – would have been 50 years**
- **Keith A – aged 16 years**

**Matthew's background**

Matthew lives alone in an isolated cottage that he rents from a farmer for whom he used to work. He suffers from chronic depression and anxiety.

He was an only child of white British parents who worked abroad. He was sent to a private boarding school in England and, although his parents wrote to him regularly, he sometimes went months without seeing them. He has told you that when he did see them they seemed like strangers who were engrossed in one another but distant with him.

He recounts to you unhappy memories from school. He found it hard to make friends and, around the age of 12, he had his first experience of uncontained anxiety. He developed unfounded fears of becoming so ill that he would not be able to see his parents. At other times he fantasised about there being no room on the train that would take him to London where he would meet them. He began to have nightmares about himself in frightening situations and one day he remembers with shame that he cried in front of other boys. He was sent to see a psychologist, and his parents were informed, but he does not remember anything coming from this.

The nightmares and other anxiety symptoms receded, and he stayed at school until he was 18. He tells you that he still found it difficult to make friends and felt too shy to talk to girls. On leaving school he started a mathematics degree at university but could not get interested in the teaching. Soon, he stopped attending lectures and spent days alone in his room. The anxious fantasies of early adolescence returned. He worried about himself, his health, his loneliness – but he turned away an offer by his tutor to put him in touch with the university counsellor.

Matthew left university before the end of the first year. For some months he lived alone in his parents' house in London and it was here that he experienced his first major episode of depression. An overwhelming sense of despair overtook his mind and this time he sought help from the GP. As a result of this he began to attend a mental health support group and it was there that he met Claire. She was a schoolteacher, also depressed, and ten years older than Matthew. He described their relationship as an 'instant experience of needing one another'.

For a while their depressions lifted and together they decided to make a new start in the countryside. Claire got a teaching job at a village school while Matthew got work as a herdsman. They lived in a cottage that went with his job. When he was 24 Claire gave birth to their son, Keith, and at the same time Matthew was asked to become the farm manager. He remembers these years as the most happy and stable in his life – though he still had depressive times and mood alterations during the day.

This situation changed abruptly when, four years ago, Claire was killed in a motor accident while returning home from school. In the months following Claire's death Matthew coped well because he had so much to do – including becoming a single parent to Keith. His employer and people in the village were supportive with childcare and other practical things. But as life settled into a routine he began once more to feel afraid and depressed, and more grief-stricken than he had felt in the months immediately following his wife's death. Slowly, he disengaged from people, even those who were trying to help him, and he lost interest in his work. His sleeping became erratic and he started to miss days from work – feeling too tired or unorganised to cope with the demands of managing the farm.

*(Continued)*

*(Continued)*

His mental health did not improve, and the antidepressants prescribed were of little benefit. Life became more and more disordered – sometimes he would spend daytimes asleep and night times awake – and mealtimes became erratic. At the request of his employer he resigned from his job but he continued to live in the cottage. His relationship with Keith became closer in the years after Claire's death but the boy's life was adversely affected by the lack of routine and disorder in the house and recently, aged 16, Keith moved to live with friends in a local town. Matthew feels that now Keith is finding his independence he can see no purpose in life on his own.

---

 **Practical work based on Case Study Two**

**Using relational theory to 'make sense' of Matthew's state of mind**

With another student –

Think about Matthew's life in terms of

1 The part played by relationships in the development of his self-identity. What links can you make between his early life experiences and his psychosocial state in adulthood?
2 Can you find any evidence that he may have moved 'away', 'against' or 'towards' others as a method of resolving childhood conflicts?
3 What experiences of 'D' needs and 'B' needs has he had in his relationships?
4 To what extent has his relationship with *himself* been influenced by his past relationships with others?

---

This is a complex case study that tells the story of a man whose emotional needs were not met in childhood. The learning to take from it is the application of concepts and ideas from relationship theory to a practical example. Theories of human relational development suggest that Matthew's childhood experiences would influence the ways in which he related to Claire and to Keith, and the ways in which he grieved her death and his son's leaving home. His experiences would also have an impact on his feelings about himself.

The study leads us into a consideration of the impact of relational attachments on our mental and physical health.

## JOHN BOWLBY AND MARY AINSWORTH

At the same time that Maslow in the United States was working out the optimal interpersonal conditions for human well-being, John Bowlby and Mary Ainsworth (an American) in the UK were exploring the same question with regard to a baby's development with its mother. Their focus was on the kind of relational attachment that would maximise the infant's mental and physical health.

Bowlby began with a model of the human infant having 'programmed inclinations' (Howe 1993: 50) to relate and attach that are based largely on the need to physically survive and feel safe. Babies have built-in behavioural abilities to elicit care from others by, for example, crying, smiling or making eye contact and, correspondingly, these actions will arouse instinctual needs in the mother to offer nurture (Bee and Boyd 2007: 266). In such conditions it is likely that a secure attachment will develop. Conversely, children whose close carers consistently respond in a non-nurturing manner are likely to engender insecure attachment patterns in their children.

The research work of Ainsworth established a typology of attachment patterns by use of the 'strange situation' in which a child between 12 and 18 months of age experiences a sequence of events that includes being left alone, and left by his or her mother in the company of an adult stranger. After this sequence of events was played out Ainsworth observed closely the behaviour of the child towards its mother. Three types of relational behaviour were categorised: the *secure*, the *insecure detached/avoidant*, and the *insecure resistant/ambivalent*.

The *secure* child will show some distress at separation from his mother and a positive response when she returns. The *insecure*, *detached* and *avoidant* child demonstrates little distress when his mother leaves and avoids contact with her on her return. The *insecure resistant* and *ambivalent* child is highly distressed at his mother's departure and not easily consoled on her return (these types are adapted from Howe 1995; Bee and Boyd 2007).

The differing relational behaviours of the children are based largely upon different relational experiences, and the behaviours are likely to become lasting personality traits. Two social work authors who were contemporaries of Bowlby and Ainsworth described the process in this way:

> the relationships an individual establishes with those who had care of him in his early days are among the most important influences that have shaped his life, because they are the patterns or prototypes of all subsequent relationships. (Ferard and Hunnybun 1972 [1962]: 13)

When Ferard and Hunnybun talk of 'prototypes' they mean what Bowlby called the *inner working model*. This describes a mental construction, a collection of ideas in the brain about the child's relationship with its primary caregiver, with itself, and its relationships with others in general (school peers, adults, extended family, etc.) Each inner working model of relationship has its corresponding relational response, such as clinging or avoidant or secure behaviour (here can be seen the similarity with Horney's ideas of a person moving towards or away from others).

Internal working models contribute towards a person's identity, and attachment theorists would expect a child who is consistently rejected to construct an inner model such as 'I'm not liked'. A model such as this can be functional insofar as it can be used by the child as a reason for not making friends, thereby not running the risk of painful rejection. But the functionality can turn into dysfunctionality in adulthood, leading to a habitual behavioural repertoire that causes loneliness, depression or anxiety.

## D.W. WINNICOTT: TRANSITIONAL OBJECTS AND TRANSITIONAL PHENOMENA

Winnicott was a contemporary of Bowlby and Ainsworth and, like them, was intrigued by the psychosocial processes that form the developing child. The phrase *transitional phenomena* derives from Winnicott's (1958 [1951]) discussion of an infant child's use of a *transitional object* in order to obtain a realistic sense of himself and his mother (carer) as persons who are separate from one another.

The assumption being made is that the newborn child occupies a highly subjective environment that is characterised by *infantile narcissism*. That is, infants have no understanding about objects existing independently of themselves so that the breast (part of mother) is experienced by the child as a part of him or self. But at some point, Winnicott says between four to 12 months, the child starts to develop its understanding about things existing outside of itself and forms an emotional, cognitive and physical attachment to its first 'other-than-me' object, thereby making the initial move away from its narcissistic world.

This psychological move, which involves a growing awareness of being dependent on things outside of the self (e.g. the 'breast – a word to be taken literally and symbolically), can create anxiety in the infant, especially when he or she first experiences the breast as not always available on demand. But, argues Winnicott, this experience is an introduction to a reality about the wider environment, and such a move is necessary for the child's healthy development because no mother can be totally attentive to her child – for even (what he called) 'good enough' parents will inevitably disappoint. He writes that

> The good enough mother ... starts off with an almost complete adaptation to her infant's needs, and as time proceeds she adapts less and less completely, gradually, according to the infant's growing ability to deal with her failure. (1958 [1951]: 238)

Her 'failure', in the sense of not being constantly available to feed and succour, introduces the child to a more general fact of life and relationships. But for the child it is a harsh fact to manage and the 'transitional object' fulfils the essential purpose of providing security while he is adapting to the idea that the breast is not part of himself, and neither is it always present for him as a source of food and comfort. The transitional or first 'not me' object mitigates the infant's anxiety. It may be a small blanket or sheet which is sucked or caressed. If the carer is absent it seems to offer comfort, a 'defence against anxiety' and becomes 'absolutely necessary...at time of loneliness or when a depressed mood threatens' (1958 [1951]: 232).

In developmental terms the key function of the transitional object is to provide the child with the experience of a psychosocial bridge which he can traverse from restricted inner reality to the 'real world'. The object (piece of blanket, etc.) is a visible reminder of the infant's invisible 'journey from the purely subjective to objectivity... the transitional object is what we see of this journey of progress towards experiencing' (1958 [1951]: 234). This 'first not-me' object to which the infant forms an attachment 'stands for' all that is outside of itself. It is illusory but, argues Winnicott, it provides a formative experience *for the remainder of life.*

Winnicott believed that the psychologically defensive strategy adopted by the developing child became a prototype that adults employed through their lives. For him the child's use of illusion to make transition is only the beginning of a process that is central to the ways in which human beings manage their inner worlds of thought and feeling when they are encountering some of life's major and most difficult transitions.

> this matter of *illusion* is one which belongs inherently to human beings and which no individual finally solves for himself or herself ... It is assumed here that the task of reality-acceptance is never completed, that no human being is free from the strain of relating inner and outer reality, and that relief from this strain is provided by an intermediate area of experience. (1958 [1951]: 240).

Winnicott gave the general title of *transitional phenomena* to the transitional objects used throughout life. They provide a way of managing the anxiety that can be present when moving from one psychosocial state to another. An example could be bereavement where a widow for a period of time after her husband's death sleeps in his pyjamas. Here she is treating an 'object', the pyjamas, 'as-if' they were something other than she knows them truly to be (Britton 1998: 58n). Projected into the object are qualities that, materially, they do not have. And, like the child's use of a comfort object, the widow's use of the pyjamas might cease as she recovers from the trauma of grief.

Human beings can also act as transitional phenomena for others, becoming temporary 'containers' during a period of psychological trauma. This is an idea to which we shall return when considering the social worker offering to clients the use of their self (Chapter 7).

## SUMMARISING THE IDEAS SO FAR

This section has made an exploration of the work of a range of influential psychosocial theorists. They hold in common the view that the individual person, with their unique combination of thoughts, feeling and behaviours, is the construction of relational experience. This experience may be symbolic insofar as a developing child may attach qualities to another thing or person that it does not, in fact, possess. You have also been given the opportunity to explore your own self-identity, seeing to what extent it links with your relational experiences, and you have tried to empathise with the identity of another.

In more recent years the psychosocial view has received empirical support from neuroscience which suggests that human brains are formed to become more or less 'social' during a 'critical period' in infancy. It is to this evidence that the chapter now turns.

## BECOMING RELATIONAL: THE BIOLOGICAL CONSTRUCTION OF THE RELATIONAL SELF

So far the focus has been on the combination of relationship influences that can be thought of as either psychological or sociological. Together these provide us with the *psychosocial* model of relational development. However, a further key element of our understanding has to be derived from the effects of relationships on the child's developing brain and how these effects can have lifelong consequences for human relating. When we incorporate the emerging data from neuroscience we end up with a *bio-psycho-social* perspective. In this model *nature is nurtured* through relational experience.

It is interaction between the baby's growing brain (nature) and his relationship experiences (nurture) that lies at the heart of his relational patterns in childhood, adolescence and adult life (Siegel 1999). In this sense, the baby's innate (biologically given) relationship propensities are shaped through psychosocial experience. Thus the infant is what Gerhardt calls an 'interactive project', an 'organism [that] has various systems ready to go, but many more that are incomplete and *will only develop in response to other human input*' (2004b: 18, my emphasis). She argues that 'the kind of brain that each baby develops is the brain that comes out of his or her experiences with other people. Love facilitates a massive burst of connections in this part of the brain between 6 and 12 months' (ibid.). During this period 'The baby is all potential. He comes with a temperament, a basic physiology and a genetic programme, but he cannot realise his potential without a particular kind of response from others...the baby has *a need* for something very specific outside himself – a maternal response' (Gerhardt 2001: 331–332).

The work of Schore (2001a, 2001b) provides social workers with what Beckett (2006: 79) calls 'a physiological basis for Bowlby's internal working model'. It points us towards understanding that the baby's fundamental need (assuming the needs for physical survival are met) is that of emotional regulation. Schore argues that in secure mother–child attachments the 'mother, at an intuitive, nonconscious level, is continuously regulating the baby's shifting arousal levels and therefore emotional states. Emotions are the highest order direct expression of bio-regulation in complex organisms, and attachment can thus be defined as the dyadic regulation of emotion' (Schore 2001a: 7). By contrast (and of crucial interest to social workers), 'Severely compromised attachment histories are...associated with brain organisations that are inefficient in regulating affective states and coping with stress' (2001a: 9).

A child whose emotions, whose anxieties and fears are soothed *before* they become traumatising is likely, in adult life, to be able to manage anxiety and stress in ways that are more functional and proportionate. A child whose carer adapts herself to the infant's emotional *flow,* who can exercise care through 'mutually attuned synchronised interactions' will go a long way towards ensuring the healthy affective development of her child (Schore 2001a: 12; also Fonagy et al. [2002: 109] on 'special moments of attunement' and Stern [1985] on 'affect attunement'). The biological perspective on attuning is provided by neuroscientists who see couples who are empathic with one another as stimulating 'similar patterns of neuronal firing' in their brains in which 'signals expressed by one person can directly stimulate corresponding systems in recipients' (Gilbert 2007: 115). Hence, carer–child attunement is a bio-psycho-social event.

Gerhardt (and others) show how parents who flow with their infants, especially during the second half of the first year of life, will help their child to develop a 'social brain' – a developed pre-frontal cortex – which goes on to play a critical part in their later ability to manage their emotional and, by implication, social lives. She argues that the child who, through early relational experience, has developed this part of the brain will be more able to pick up on social cues, non-verbal messages from others, to empathise, and be able to restrain primitive emotional impulses (Gerhardt 2004a).

Thus, it can be seen that the 'transacting' process or 'dance' of 'intersubjectivity' (Gilbert 2007: 25) between the nurturing, empathic relationship offered by the carer, and the baby's brain development, leads to the growing child's ability to become more empathic, with emerging relational skills. Schore claims for these linkages 'a direct relationship between an enabling socioemotional environment, an optimally developing brain, and adaptive infant mental health' (2001a: 5).

Given this emerging knowledge base from neuroscience, and taking it in conjunction with psychosocial theory, we are now able to say with confidence that who we are, and who we become, are in very large part creations of the relationships that have been part of our life. This early and critical period of relational experience will influence all our subsequent relationships. It is, writes Siegel (1999: 21), these relationships that 'literally shape the structure of the child's developing brain'. It seems that it is impossible to overestimate the significance of this relational formation to social life, individual contentment and fulfilment. As Gerhardt says, 'the kind of brain that each baby develops is the brain that comes out of his or her particular experiences with people' (2004b: 38). And this is why the study and the experience of relationships are of inestimable importance to the social work profession.

## RELATIONSHIPS AND THE CREATION OF PATHOLOGY

Just as relationships can create happiness (Argyle 1987), and happiness may, in turn, promote physical health (Salovey et al. 2000), so poor relationships can create chronic mental disorders characterised by anxiety, melancholy and, possibly, severe psychopathology. If an infant experiences relational trauma then, later in life, his capacity to develop and maintain interpersonal relationships, cope with stress, and regulate emotion, is impaired (Schore 2001b). Schore refers to such a person as having an 'enduring deficit' (2001b: 9) in his ability to manage new, and therefore stressful, emotional experiences.

Kohut goes so far as to suggest that '*all* forms of psychopathology' or 'flaws in the self are due to disturbances of ... relationships in childhood' (1984: 53 my emphasis). Kahn (1997) reinforces the point, arguing that if a child does not receive adequate therapeutic mirroring and empathic *acceptance* from the parent, then development is impaired and the emerging personality is marked by insecurity, uncertainty about the self and its acceptability to others.

Traumatising influences can be pre-birth. Gerhardt writes about the baby in the womb becoming *predisposed* to stress:

> It is not really surprising that the foetus is so vulnerable to the mother's state of mind and body, since her body is temporarily the body of the foetus. Her dietary deficiencies and her stress levels become his. This means that she can pass on – by non-genetic means – her own oversensitised stress response to her baby. (2004b: 67)

A similar point is made by Schore who brings together research to demonstrate that the infant's brain development during the third trimester of pregnancy can be chemically affected in ways that will go on to affect the child's later relational patterns, producing 'an enduring neurophysiological vulnerability' (2001b: 5). He continues by discussing the 'detrimental effects of maternal alcohol, drug and tobacco use during pregnancy' that are associated with 'poor infant interactive capacities' (ibid: 5).

This kind of data about the transmission of mental states between mother and born or unborn child is one example of the general proposition that relationships, whether positive and life enhancing, or damaging and diminishing to life's chances, have a large and lasting impact upon our lives. Of particular interest to social workers, whose raw material is often people's distressed, distressing and problematic behaviour, is the strong evidence from the psychosocial and the neuroscience data that early relational trauma is likely to have adverse and, possibly, lifelong mental and behavioural effects upon those who experience it.

Of course, social workers more than most people will know that no one has had a 'perfect' childhood, and they may have had their interest in the profession first aroused by abusive or neglectful relationships in their own lives. But, in such adverse circumstances, the significance for personal development and professional practice is not *what* has happened to you in the past, but what *use* you have made of what has happened. The important questions to ask of the self are: have I become truly self-aware about the effects on me of my relational history, and will I be able to use this self-awareness appropriately and creatively as a resource in my professional relationships? In later chapters we shall return to this topic by using the idea of the 'wounded healer' (Nouwen 1979) – the person who has managed (perhaps with professional help) to convert their own wounded state into a source of therapy for their clients.

## MAPPING YOUR PERSONAL RELATIONAL IDENTITY

It has been argued that critical dimensions of our mental, social, physical and behavioural lives are either enhanced or impaired by our relational experiences. To a large extent our identity has been, and is being, constructed and maintained by our relationships with others.

Most of us occupy a matrix of relationships that are expressed and linked through physical touch, through our thoughts and feelings and our social connections. We live in a network of others, some with intimacy, some at a distance. For most of us the network is composed of our close or extended family, our friends, work colleagues, fellow students, neighbours, the people whom we pay for services (plumbers, dentists …), and so on.

Of course, the clients of social workers also occupy a relational matrix. For many their relational experiences have impaired their psychological and social functioning. Those who are users of the services for families and children have often endured abuse and relationship breakdown. Likewise, the users of the mental health services can find that their mental disorder is either the cause or the effect of relationship loss and separation. Older people, too, can be deeply affected by loss and the enforced change of personal identity that is associated with, for example, the deaths of others or moving into residential or nursing care.

---

### Exercise Two

**Attachment maps and relational identity: constructing a personal emotional matrix**

In the following practical exercise you are asked to construct an emotional matrix of your relational identity. The purpose of the exercise is to increase your awareness of

- relationships in your life;
- their significance, or lack of significance, to your emotional self;
- whether the relationships are configured in the way that meets your emotional needs;
- or whether you would alter them if you could.

**Part 1 (Done alone)**

1   Take a sheet of paper and work on your own. Write your name in the centre and around your name write the names of others (family, friends, acquaintances, and so on). Position the names of the others either close to or further away from your name, according to how *emotionally close* you feel to them. For example, your brother might live thousands of miles away but, if you feel 'close' to him, position him close to your name. Conversely, you might live in the same house as another person and not feel close. Position this person further away. When you have finished you will have constructed your personal matrix that starts to measure *emotional* proximity.

2   We sometimes have relationships that are difficult to position. For example, you might feel that someone *ought* to be positioned close to you, but you also feel that you need them to be at a distance. Or you might feel ambivalent about a person, sometimes close and sometimes distant. Become aware of people for whom it is difficult to make a positioning decision. You might resolve this difficulty by putting their name in two different places.

*(Continued)*

*(Continued)*

**Part 2 (Done with a partner)**

- Discuss your matrix and (as much as you choose to) say why you have positioned people where they are.
- Would you ideally want to move them further away?
- Or would you like to move them closer?
- Do you have any sense of being emotionally *held* by this relational matrix?
- Do you have any sense of using your *self* to hold others?

**Learning points from constructing your emotional matrix**

- The exercise is devised to increase your awareness of yourself as an attached person within your human context.
- You should be able to use the matrix to identify your needs to relate to others and, probably, their needs to relate to you.
- Linked with this, you should get an idea of how your *self* meets the needs of others, and how you can *use* your self for this purpose (for example, by texting a friend, sending a birthday card or inviting them to join your Facebook).
- Overall, you might get a sense of being *held* by others in a human, social and emotional scaffolding, and you playing your part in holding others.
- This sense of using yourself for others, and holding others, will be used throughout the book as a model of what relationship based social workers may do for their clients.

## RELATIONSHIPS MATTER TO HUMANITY – AND THEREFORE TO SOCIAL WORKERS

In writing this chapter what has impressed itself most on my mind is that many major personality and developmental theorists, while differing in other ways, agree on the core proposition that relationships have the power to enhance or diminish the person – to build up or destroy a person's self-identity, their self-esteem, their ability to relate to others in secure, honest, and 'being' (Maslow 1968) ways.

So, whether it be Erikson, Horney, Maslow, Bowlby, Schore or Gerhardt, it can be seen that developing infants are relationship seekers, love seekers. In their seeking they are attempting to evolve what several of the theorists call the 'self' or 'being': the inner and authentic core that marks out the true 'me'. This core drives towards finding its 'identity', flourishing if it encounters a love that enhances its existence. But whether or not it discovers and activates its true innate capacities is almost completely dependent on the ways in which it experiences relations with significant others. The response that children get to their seeking will affect profoundly what happens in their futures, sometimes to the point where their seeking stops because it brings only emotional pain.

It is precisely the critical impact that relationships have upon the human condition that makes it essential that social workers not only interest themselves in them, but work with them, and interact with their clients within them, trying always to enrich the client–worker engagement. But very often social workers are faced with clients whose chances of self-realisation have been severely limited by their early life experiences. In situations like this it is not that the client's underlying need to love and be loved, the wanting relational contact, has gone away. Rather, the problem arises that the need becomes expressed in ways that are unsatisfying, ineffective and, possibly, anti-social. Following Horney's conceptual framework, as social workers we might see an acutely insecure client attempting to find psychological safety by dominating and exploiting others (moving against – possibly in an abusive way), or by avoiding the society of others (moving away), or by seeking protection from others (moving towards – possibly to the point of becoming a victim of abuse). Similarly, in the language of attachment, relational patterns characterised by avoidance or by clinging may be indicative of deep anxiety about the linkages between the self and the other.

While social workers must make appropriate judgements about these kinds of behaviours, and act decisively to protect the vulnerable, the worker who is also practising in a relational manner will distinguish the *person* from the behaviour. The relational social worker understands that these behaviours are often symptomatic of damaging relational experiences in the past (this is the assessment/analytical aspect of relationship based practice) and he or she will offer their own self as a relational and, possibly, reparative resource for their client.

Of course, this professional relationship might be accepted, rejected, ridiculed or abused. The relationship offering might disturb a client's equilibrium, threatening their precarious psychosocial safety. But a skilled, sensitive relational social worker will understand the responses of his or her client, not take them personally and, sometimes, will be able to use them in a way that helps the client towards self-awareness and healing.

This kind of relationship based practice is attempting to be therapeutic – a word and activity which means working in such a way that benign, healing change is facilitated in the client. The social worker's offering of him or herself does not rely on analytical cleverness – but it does require the practitioner to become self-aware and to activate their caring instincts by listening empathically and acting practically in the interests of the client.

Future chapters will focus upon how the worker prepares him or her self for this kind of relational work.

## CHAPTER SUMMARY

- Our adult personalities (our patterns of thinking, feeling and behaving) are largely a result of our early relational experiences.
- This finding is supported by the convergence of psychological, sociological and biological theory.

- Because relationships are so influential in our formation, they become of critical importance to social work.
- Social workers are relationally formed beings, just like their clients. Their self-awareness about their relational experiences is important if they are to practise relationally with their clients.
- The chapter has also provided you with opportunities to apply the theoretical ideas to your own life, thus enhancing your awareness of your relational experiences in the past and the present.

 *Further reading*

Gerhardt, S. (2004) *Why Love Matters: how affection shapes a baby's brain.* Hove: Brunner-Routledge.
This book distils in a readable way much of the neuroscience which shows how our brains are formed by our earliest relationships.

Goffman, E. (1990 [1959]) *The Presentation of Self in Everyday Life.* London: Penguin.
A psychosocial classic in which Goffman shows how our transactions with others are shaped by learned and expected behavioural roles or 'performances'.

Maslow, A. (1968), *Towards a Psychology of Being.* Princeton, NJ: Van Nostrand.
In Parts 1 and 2 of this book Maslow sets out his understanding of humanity, its deepest needs, and his hopefulness about human development.

Sudbery, J. (2002) 'Key features of therapeutic social work: the use of relationship', *Journal of Social Work Practice, 16 (2).*
In this article Sudbery emphasises the social worker's use of relationships, approaching the topic from a therapeutic and psychodynamic understanding.

# 4   KNOWING AND USING ONESELF IN RELATIONSHIP BASED SOCIAL WORK

## INTRODUCTION

The last chapter set out the theoretical bases for believing that relationships and, in particular, the emotions that underpin them, play a critical part in our bio-psycho-social formation during childhood and throughout our adult lives. As these knowledge bases grow, and we become increasingly aware of the critical impact of relationships, both positive and negative, on our lives, social workers are led towards a fundamental question about professional practice. That is, how can they *use* this knowledge about the effects of relationships in a way that both benefits their clients and meets their practice objectives?

The implication here is that relational theory should be 'matched' (Ward and McMahon 1998) by relational practice. That is, using the theory that relationships are critical to human development implies the practical, relational *use of the self* within client–worker encounters. In this way social workers personally enact the theory, and such relating, in a disciplined, informed, compassionate and purposeful manner, is what 'relationship based practice' means.

Previous chapters have shown that relationship based practice requires a combination of both *inter*personal and *intra*personal skills. This chapter will concentrate on the intrapersonal, looking into the self and discovering why self-awareness is so important, and how it is acquired. This learning and process of self-discovery are the bases for meeting Key Role 1, Element 1.3, to

- Reflect on your own background, experiences and practice that may have an impact on the relationship.
- Review the likely impact of your own … role and responsibilities in the relationship (NOS Key Roles).

The idea of self-awareness will also be located within the broader structure of social work, so that it becomes clear how it is linked with theory, practice and values.

## THE PROBLEMS OF DEFINING SELF-AWARENESS

In Chapter 2 the benefits of self-awareness in the social worker were emphasised and short case studies were provided to illustrate practically the theoretical ideas. But while it is easy to say that social workers should be self-aware it is difficult, and probably impossible, to define *exactly* what this means. The problem arises from our requiring self-awareness in order to study self-awareness (Beitman and Nair 2004). Put simply, we encounter an oft-faced dilemma for social scientists: that we cannot stand outside of ourselves and be 'objective'. We are that which we are trying to study.

Jopling (2000) observes that there is a further difficulty insofar as a person's *claiming* to know himself is not enough to assure us that *in fact* he does know himself. The human propensity for self-deception, deliberate or accidental, is too great. Thus, Jopling argues that self-awareness is a condition which is acquired through the disciplines of reflective self-enquiry and self-evaluation. Such processes lead to a person knowing

> with some acuity the shape and development of their moral personality, the direction their lives are taking, and the values that matter most to them... [they are people] who have achieved a level of personal integrity through the adoption of a stance of self-criticism toward their immediate desires, beliefs and volitions; and who have not accepted uncritically any conventional and ready-to-hand forms of self-understanding as descriptive of the true nature of the self, but who have, by reasoning, choice, dialogue, or moral reflection, arrived at their own ways of making sense of themselves and their life histories. (Jopling 2000: 2)

Jopling's description is helpful for social workers. It is not making anything mystical out of self-awareness, but it is presenting it as a condition that is only found and maintained by personal work. It should be seen as a process without end, never an absolute or arrival at a one-off state. It is ever partial, altering as life develops and, for the reason given by Beitman and Nair (2004), always imperfect. In a sentence that seems applicable to the social work profession Jopling suggests that 'those who are self-knowledgeable are better equipped for the practical...duties of life than those who suffer from self-deception', for such a state undermines the 'development of related virtues such as integrity, political and moral responsibility, and self-direction' (2000: 4–5).

With the ideas of Beitman and Nair and Jopling in mind the phrase 'self-aware social worker' should be understood as describing a relative condition. In other words, one social worker may be more self-aware than another, while the perfectly self-aware social worker can never exist. But what exactly does self-awareness offer to social workers, and why should they make the effort to achieve it?

When social workers achieve a high standard of self-awareness they become more able to provide to themselves (and others) an accurate account of their motivations, the reasons why they are acting, feeling and thinking in certain ways. And, of equal importance, self-aware social workers who *cannot* provide such an account know that they cannot. Their self-awareness helps them to know that they are confused, that they have not understood, and such states of mind trouble them. Through their discipline of self-enquiry they seek understanding, they ponder upon events, trying to discover what is confusing their thoughts and feelings.

Such a state of being stands in stark contrast to the worker whose actions spring from causes of which she is ignorant, whose thoughts and feelings emerge in a seemingly random and disconnected way. This social worker may not be able to understand herself because she does not have the tools to do so, or because she has not acquired the discipline of self-enquiry.

A short case study will help to illustrate the point.

 **Case Study One**

Imagine that you work in a community based, older persons team. You accept a new referral to assess the needs of an elderly man who is living alone in his own home.

On your first visit you feel uneasy with this man and, as time passes and you work your way through the assessment process, the feelings become stronger. Quite involuntarily, you take a dislike to your client, and you leave his house without becoming involved in any 'small talk'.

**The self-aware and the self-unaware social worker**

If you are a self-aware social worker you will be interested in your feelings and where they have come from. You will try to analyse this meeting and what it was that provoked such emotions in you. Your striving for self-awareness means that you will not take your feelings at face value. Rather you will try to dig below the surface to make sense of them, to explain why you feel one way and not another.

By contrast, the non-self-aware social worker will tend to accept uncritically her feelings, without trying to pinpoint accurately what underlies them. She will probably attribute her emotions to her client, seeing in him something unknown that creates unease within her.

The distinction being made here is that while the self-aware social worker might say 'I felt uneasy in that situation' the non-self-aware social worker is more likely to say 'He made me feel uneasy'. Behind this choice of words lie radically different approaches because the first worker is taking some responsibility for her feelings while the second is holding the client responsible.

This case study can be thought about under the four headings of *theory, practice, values* and *self*.

## Theory

Social work theory is concerned with making analytical sense of human situations. It seeks to explain complex human circumstances and when the social worker is theorising she cannot reasonably exclude herself from the explanation because she is part of the circumstances about which she is trying to make sense. To the extent that she is self-aware, she will be able to disentangle and become clear about the effects that she is having on the situation, and the effects the situation is having on her. Such clarity is critical for accurate case assessment.

## Practice

When theoretical understandings are accurate, then practical interventions are more likely to meet the client's true needs. A social worker who attributes the sole cause of her uneasiness to her client, without examining her own inner world and why she feels what she feels, is less likely to see her client as he truly is. She is likely to project on to him unexplored feelings that are within her, to associate him with things that, in truth, he has no connection with. In such psychologically confused circumstances this worker's practical intervention, perhaps only in small and unnoticeable ways, will be distorted by her emotional state.

Having said this, and by contrast, social workers have long been aware of what is sometimes called 'practice wisdom'. It is usually thought of as being acquired through experience and based on intuitive aspects of the mind which, although without strong empirical evidence, are able to 'sense' that there is 'something wrong' in a situation. In such circumstances (and especially in safeguarding situations) it is proper for a worker, without prejudice to a client, to discuss her felt concern with a colleague or in supervision. Such a discussion could reveal that the feeling of 'uneasiness' is rooted in the external situation and not entirely within the worker. Rustin's (2005) discussion of attending to 'gut feelings' in child protection cases (referred to in the next chapter) makes a similar point.

## Values

With regard to values, social workers seek to treat their clients equitably, with fairness and justice, and as individuals. If they are to act in these ways it is essential that they see in their client the real or true person, and not an object that is blurred by their own confused emotions. Self-awareness is the key to such clarity of vision and for this reason it is one of the foundations of value based social work.

## Self

The key learning point from this imaginary case is that your ability and discipline to *work with yourself* underpins your ability to apply social work theory, to practise in a way that meets your client's true needs, and work within a values framework. Becoming a self-aware social worker is the basis for becoming a theoretically capable and values based relational practitioner.

Paradoxically, it seems that the explored *subjectivity* of the social worker leads to *objectivity* which is the basis for accurate and just assessments. If you as a worker know yourself you are likely to have clearer and more veridical perceptions about others. Thus it should not be thought that a social worker's disciplined search for self-awareness clouds issues. On the contrary, it opens up the best chance of achieving accurate assessment and compassionate involvement because it frees a worker to see things as they are.

## THE SUBJECTIVE SELF – AND KNOWING IT

When you relate to your clients, *who you are* becomes a part of the practice. There is what England (1986: 35) called a 'pervasive use of self' running through social work – you inevitably bring your personality into the situation (Howe: 1998). This is why Clare Winnicott wrote that 'those who want to understand other people ... have to be prepared to understand themselves' (in Kanter 2004: 227) and, on this topic, there is a longstanding consensus in the social work literature (for example Goldberg 1953, Irvine 1966, among many others).

So the more social workers learn about themselves, the more aware they become of the life experiences that have formed them, of why they habitually think, feel and behave in the ways that they do – and the more ready they are to become skilled relational practitioners. This kind of learning can only come about by a process of self-discovery, undertaken on your own and with others.

The following exercise will help to enhance your self-awareness.

---

**Exercise One**

**The genogram**

A genogram is similar to a family tree. Below you will see an example which would of course require adapting to your circumstances.

Some people never knew their parents, or perhaps knew or know one and not the other. Likewise, family separations, early deaths, families losing touch, or geographical mobility, may mean that little or nothing is known about grandparents.

Sometimes children have been brought up separately from their natural parents, either in the care system or as adoptees. For them, a genogram will be very different, both practically and experientially.

All genograms are unique. There is no one who is the same as you, and it is for this reason that your professional social work practice will always differ, if only slightly, from that of colleagues in your team.

Constructing this genogram is a further exercise in discovering who you are in the disciplined fashion that is the essential basis for relationship based social work.

Before you begin your own genogram it would help you to look at Figure 4.1. It relates to Sophie, the imaginary social work student whose life is explored in the LIFELINE diagrams throughout the book.

*(Continued)*

---

(Continued)

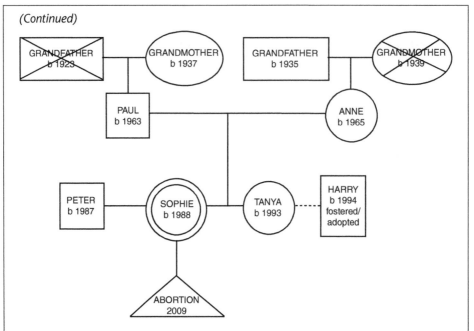

**Figure 4.1** Sophie: Genogram

Sophie's genogram is relatively easy to set out by using symbols. The subject of the diagram (Sophie in this case) is symbolised by a double circle or, if male, a double square. When you construct your own genogram you may require symbols for other types of relationships such as cohabitation, divorced couples, twins, stillbirths, and so on. Below are given some of the ways of representing these relationships, and you can find a fuller discussion about the uses of genograms in social work in Parker and Bradley (2003) and Miller (2006). Not all symbols used in genograms are universally agreed and you may need to make up your own, or simply add in writing what may be an unusual relationship.

**Some frequently used genogram symbols**

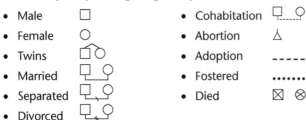

**Part 1 (Done alone)**

1 Using a large sheet of paper and the frequently used symbols construct your personal genogram.
2 Write in people's first names and dates of birth if you know them.

3  If people have died, write in the date of death if you know it.

4  Write in dates of marriages, separations and divorces.

5  Each family is unique and if circumstances are unusual you may have to invent your own symbol or describe the situation in words.

**Part 2 (Done with a partner)**

- When you have completed your genogram find a partner to work with and show it to them. Now talk with them about particular aspects of it that stand out for you.
- Next, think in particular of *one* person in your genogram. Tell your partner about him or her, and why you chose them to talk about.
- Now, think about the people in your extended family and tell your partner if you 'see yourself' in any of them.
- Are you similar, different, or *deliberately* different to those you spent your child-hood with?
- Does anything about the history of individuals in your family help you to understand why you have chosen social work as a career?

The purpose of constructing your genogram is to learn more about the self that you will take with you into your professional practice. Just as an engineer 'knows' his tools, so you should know the tool that you are, for, in a real sense, 'you' are what you will use in your practice.

The genogram is an intensely subjective exercise, and now is the time for you to begin locating your subjective self within the more objective framework of social work theory, practice and values.

## LOCATING THE SELF WITHIN THE BROADER CONTEXT OF SOCIAL WORK

You have begun a disciplined intrapersonal process of knowing yourself. Now it becomes important to see how your subjective self fits into an objective understanding of social work.

Professional training for social work is usually based upon three discrete but interrelated dimensions: theory, practice, and values. Theory is concerned with explaining human situations that might otherwise puzzle us (Payne 2005, Beckett 2006, Howe 2009). It is the knowledge base of social work that helps us to make sense of what we meet in practice, providing the concepts with which we may understand complex human behaviour and ways of relating. Social workers have available to them a range of theories, some with accompanying therapies. For example, cognitive behavioural *theory* explains how we sometimes 'think' our way into feeling depressed or anxious, and cognitive behavioural *therapy* is a practical intervention that helps us to interrupt our thoughts when they become irrational and conducive to a depressed or anxious mood.

Practice is concerned with skilled social work action (e.g. interviewing, assessing, communicating, empathic listening, managing emotions, self-reflection, etc.) that is guided by theory (Trevithick 2005, Koprowska 2008). The example above from CBT could be used by a social worker in a community mental health team. Equally, a social worker who finds humanistic ideas more persuasive or effective may apply the theory by using person-centred methods of being with her client.

Values are concerned with the ethical bases of theory and practice (e.g. codes of conduct such as those of BASW, GSCC (General Social Care Council), IFSW, and see Banks 2006, Banks and Gallagher 2009). Often they tell us *why* we should practise in one way rather than another. They may be the dimensions of social work education about which most emotion is felt because values may be associated with the deeper and most personal meanings of our lives.

This theory, practice and values triad is comprehensive insofar as it includes the cognitive (analysing), the practical (doing) and, perhaps, some emotional dimensions (values about which you *feel*) of the individual student. However, as a student, your learning is often focused upon the third person (i.e. the client) only. This means that you acquire theories *about others*, you develop practice skills to use *with others*, and you adopt values in relation *to others*. From the perspective of relationship based practice and the use of self this third person type of education, crucial as it is to professional training and objectivity, requires the complementary addition of the subjective, first person perspective – thus turning the theory, practice, values triad away from others and towards the self. Hence, you would apply *theory* (such as developmental psychology) to *yourself* as well as others. Developing the skill of being reflectively and mindfully with yourself would complement the *practice* 'people skills' (such as empathy and listening) that you acquire. And *values* teaching, in addition to the adoption of professional codes and attitudes towards others, would be a personal exploration of those matters that are of ultimate importance to you, the individual student or social worker.

Without such a personalisation, professional training risks becoming learning that is restricted to the outer world of other people and, as such, takes no account of the individual student who is destined to become the professional knower, practitioner and holder of values. At worst you, the student, are treated like 'a space through which something else passes' (Tillich 1964: 136) rather than a human subject who will be attempting to mediate your new learning through your life experiences, your beliefs and your cognitive and emotional states.

Thus, as well as projecting what is learned in college on to the outside world, it is introjected into the self. This leads to the fourth dimension of social work training.

## THE FOURTH DIMENSION

To the three dimensions of social work must be added a fourth which is that of the *self*. In the last chapter the self was presented as the personality of the individual social worker, the unique constellation of feelings, thoughts and behaviours that is based upon his genetic inheritance, his life and relational experiences, and the value choices he has made.

It is precisely the uniqueness of each individual social worker that will cause him to engage with and interpret theory, practice and values in ways that are distinctive to him. His life experiences, past and present, and his cognitive-emotional reactions to them, are likely to influence his orientation to social work theory, his practical ways of enacting theory, and his ethical motivation or value system.

In the triangular diagram below (Figure 4.2) you can imagine yourself, your *unique* self, in the centre (write your name there). On the outside of you are social work theory, practice skills and values, some of which, during the course of your professional development, you will internalise and make 'your own'. This internalisation will go towards constructing your professional 'self'.

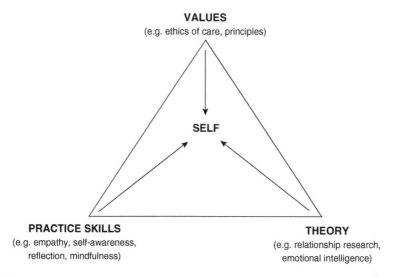

**VALUES**
(e.g. ethics of care, principles)

**SELF**

**PRACTICE SKILLS**
(e.g. empathy, self-awareness,
reflection, mindfulness)

**THEORY**
(e.g. relationship research,
emotional intelligence)

**Figure 4.2**

The corner of the triangle entitled 'Practice Skills' includes empathy, self-awareness and personal reflection. It is these skills and states of being, awareness of self and empathy with the other person, that lie at the heart of relationship based practice.

The 'Theory' corner of the triangle is focused upon becoming familiar with research that points to the critical importance of the relationship for human development. This is the knowledge base of relational practice. You may need to refer back to the last chapter to remind yourself of the bio-psycho-social bases of this knowledge. The next chapter extends that theory base by examining the role of emotional intelligence in relationship based practice and the use of self.

The 'Values' corner of the 'Use of self' triangle is concerned with ethical principles, altruism, virtues and the ethics of care – the topics of Chapter 7.

In all social work practice there is interaction between theory, practice, values and self – each of these influencing the others. And the end result of any particular social work intervention will always be, to a greater or lesser extent, unique, because the subjective self of the social worker mediates the more objective dimensions of theory and practice.

## SELF-AWARENESS AND THE IMPLEMENTATION OF THEORY, PRACTICE AND VALUES

The skilled task of the relationship based practitioner is to use her subjective self within the more objectively defined frameworks of social work theory, practice and values.

Within statutory social work, and particularly where risk assessment is involved, the crucial part played by self-awareness may be demonstrated by thinking about a situation where a social worker is *not* aware of herself, where she is *unaware* of her feelings, or perhaps *denying* her feelings (refer back to Freud in Chapter 3) and what lies behind her behaviour. In such circumstances serious confusion and perhaps even damage can ensue. This may be particularly true if the hard to manage emotions such as sexual attraction, anger, anxiety or deep distress are engendered by the client–worker relationship.

It is in circumstances such as these that Ferguson (2005) discusses the temptations for a social worker to *avoid* a relationship as a way of reducing his or her own anxieties. The exercise that follows is adapted from Ferguson's work.

---

### Exercise Two

**The emotional self, and self-deception in the face of anxiety**

Imagine a child protection worker in a Family Intervention Services team. She has a large caseload and many of the parents whose children are subjects of child protection plans do not welcome her involvement. From time to time she and her colleagues experience verbal abuse and, occasionally, threats of physical violence.

Working in this atmosphere increases her anxiety in two ways. Firstly, she is there to protect children and she worries if she is doing her job well. And secondly, she worries about her own security.

With one particularly threatening family, and without really being aware of what she is doing, she develops a strategy that relieves her worries. She begins to write to the parents to announce her visits. The effect of this is that they are forewarned of her coming and they and the child usually leave the house before she arrives.

In order to make sure that she sees the child she could revert to the unannounced visits that she used to make. But, instead, she continues to write and the parents continue to leave the house before she visits.

---

## Points to consider

1 In terms of self-awareness, what is happening in this situation? It seems that, for reasons that she does not fully understand, the social worker is engaging in self-deception and self-defence.
2 The self-deception arises because she is, perhaps, persuading herself that she is doing her job properly.
3 The self-defence arises from her avoidance of a situation that she finds threatening.
4 Her objectivity about the situation and discharging her statutory duties appear to be swamped by her subjective feelings of anxiety.

## Questions to discuss

1 What are the obstacles to this social worker becoming aware of the true reasons behind writing letters to arrange appointments?
2 Could she become self-aware and do her job properly?
3 What support would she need in order to work in a less defensive way?

These are difficult questions to answer. The first thing to note is that remaining self-aware in social work is challenging. Thompson (2005: 90) takes the view that without self-awareness social workers can become ingrained in their ways and, potentially, 'out of touch with reality'. However, we should also be aware that becoming out of touch with reality can become a comforting position, just as it seems to have done with the social worker in this example.

Real life examples of self-comforting and reduced self-awareness can be found in Rustin's (2005) analysis of the death of Victoria Climbié. She discusses workers' failures to pay attention to their 'gut feelings' about the case, of putting them to one side because not to do so would bring discomfort and more work. She describes this self-defensive way of working as 'mindlessness' – 'the failure to keep things in mind, to make connections and have a perspective that connects past and present', leading to a worker's 'fragmented sense of self'. And if the worker's internal reality is fragmented, so too will be external reality. Objectivity will be obscured and accurate assessment impaired.

By contrast, Rustin advocates training for 'mindfulness' – a theory and a practice for social workers that 'allows them to perceive such levels of distress and have a context in which they can assess its impact on them'. In similar vein Reder and Duncan (2003), discussing flawed inter-agency communications in serious child abuse cases, make reference to workers' 'psychological processes, such as anxiety, which inhibit thinking' and they stress the importance of becoming aware of the 'impact of factors in oneself or in the case on one's ability to think'. More recently, Howe reiterates the point when he writes that:

> Before the worker can be in touch with the feelings of the client, she must first be able to acknowledge and understand her own emotional states and the power they have to affect her, particularly as she relates with others in need, distress, anger and despair. (2008: 185)

The risk being discussed here is summarised by Miller's (2006: 39) concern that social workers might act in ways that are 'more about our own needs than those of service users'. For her, the guard against this happening is self-awareness.

For social workers to remain self-aware, and not fall into the potentially danger-ous practice that has been discussed above, their processes of acquiring and retain-ing self-awareness must become part and parcel of their normal activities of practice (in Chapter 6 methods of retaining self-awareness, including mindfulness and professional supervision, will be discussed).

In the example a routine engagement in the process of self-awareness would have led the worker, either on her own or with a skilled colleague or superviser, to name her feelings, to say what it is that is threatening. And, after developing a vocabulary that truly describes her self, she would be helped to make sense of her emotional state. Fear is sometimes confined to one situation, a so-called specific fear, but at other times fears are felt across different aspects of life. The social worker should be encouraged to reflect more generally on her life, on her relationships, and to become aware of other anxiety-provoking circumstances, either from the past, in the present, or the anticipated future.

Of course, this kind of process temporarily renders a worker emotionally vulner-able. By its nature it has the effect of reducing her defences by opening up areas of her life that may be sensitive and fragile. But the result of the process may be strengthening. She will know herself better and therefore be better placed to *use her self* in her work. Her mind will be more attuned to the emotional dimensions of life but in such a way that the attunement does not make her over-defensive. She is in a process of becoming what has been called a 'wounded healer' (Nouwen 1979)– one who has entered into her hurt state at such a depth of honesty that, paradoxically, she acquires the strength, the courage and the skills to help others to do the same.

To work in this self-aware way social workers need supportive teams and supportive managers. The following example helps to illustrate the point.

---

   **Case Study Two**

The mother of a middle-aged social worker from an older persons team is showing the early signs of dementia. He feels sad for his mother and anxious for himself. His father had Alzheimer's before he died a few years ago. Does this mean that he, like his parents, is destined to suffer from brain disease?

Previously the social worker had not taken a special interest in dementia but now he starts to read more about it, thus building up his knowledge base.

He also describes his feelings of sadness and fear to a colleague. In this way he opens up his emotional state to another person but, just as importantly, he opens it up to himself. Naming and facing his emotions, bringing them out into the open, makes them feel more manageable and he feels less vulnerable to the anxious thoughts that had pervaded his mind.

His professional practice alters too as he becomes aware of his increased sensitivity to, and compassion for, dementia sufferers. He questions his personal value base, and ethical concepts such as 'dignity' and 'respect' take on an enhanced significance for him.

Now, when he meets clients suffering from dementia his personal experiences with his parents, and the ways in which he has responded to them, free him to listen to their worries. He had been afraid that his experiences would make him defensive with dementia sufferers, anxious that their experiences would activate his own delicate emotional state. Of course, his feelings are still within him. But now they have become a source of empathy with others, leading to a reaching out rather than the closing down that can result from anxiety.

His quest for self-awareness through introspection has freed him to experience the outer world less fearfully, engaging more fully with his own anxieties and those of others. His looking inward with honesty has become the basis for looking outward with honesty. He is using his inner world, 'using himself' for others.

The case illustrates the way in which a social worker's personal history, and particularly his *relational* history, can affect the theoretical understanding and practical outcomes of his work. In this instance the emotions that are experienced in connection with adverse changes in a personal relationship influence what professional theory, knowledge and values come to prominence in his mind. His personal self is entering into and affecting his professional practice. This social worker is 'using himself' by offering something of 'who he is' to his clients.

Using the self in a disciplined, knowledgeable and purposeful manner, far from being a minor aside to the practical business of meeting clients' needs, allocating resources, assessing risks or dealing with emergencies, is the professional foundation upon which we can perform these social work activities – for without awareness of the self, and the using of this self in relationship, social work activity is reduced to impersonal service delivery.

## A DEEPER EXPLORATION OF YOUR LIFE IN RELATION TO PROFESSIONAL PRACTICE

The NOS require you to reflect on your own background, experiences and practice that may have an impact on relationships with clients. You have made a start on this reflective process and have learned that the self-awareness that comes through personal reflection is a continuing requirement of your professional development.

The last chapter showed that who we have become has been influenced in large part by our relationships and life experiences. It therefore follows that when social workers use themselves in their professional practice they are bringing to bear on the present time all that their past has made them. In ways that cannot be measured workers will transfer into the present moment the attitudes, beliefs, behavioural mannerisms and ways of seeing things that have been internalised from their infancy onwards.

But, although this is true, human beings are not only passive receivers of their past relationships and experiences. They have self-volition in their lives. To some degree each of us can choose the ways in which we relate to others and respond to our environment. The following exercise of constructing your personal LIFELINE will enable you to track the course of your life and identify the influences that have shaped who you are. You will be able to pinpoint pivotal points in your life, decisions that were made by you or by others that have altered the course that life has taken.

The personal LIFELINE exercise is in several stages which will continue in further chapters of the book. You are therefore asked to keep it in a safe place and, because it will eventually become a large document, you are advised to start it on a sheet of A3 paper.

---

**Exercise Three**

**Your personal LIFELINE**

The LIFELINE exercise is done in several stages. The purpose is to continue the process of building up your self-awareness in preparation for professional practice. You are asked to follow the instructions carefully, and in Stage 1 not to add anything that is not factual (see below).

Throughout the book you will find example diagrams of a LIFELINE in five stages. It relates to the life of Sophie, an imaginary social work student. The first version (LIFELINE 1 on the following page) shows you how to start building your own LIFELINE diagram, although you will be able to add many more facts than are shown on the example.

**Exercise 3(A): constructing your LIFELINE 1 (Done alone)**

- Take a large sheet of paper (A3 preferably) and draw a wavy line from one corner to the corner diagonally opposite.
- At the top of the line write your date of birth.
- At the bottom of the line write the word 'NOW'.
- Near to where you have entered your date of birth write the names of the family that you were born into (if you have this information). Name your parent(s) and any older brothers or sisters, with their years of birth.
- Now begin to enter the 'facts' of your life, using the LIFELINE as a chronology and positioning the facts on the line in proportion to when they occurred between your birth and NOW.

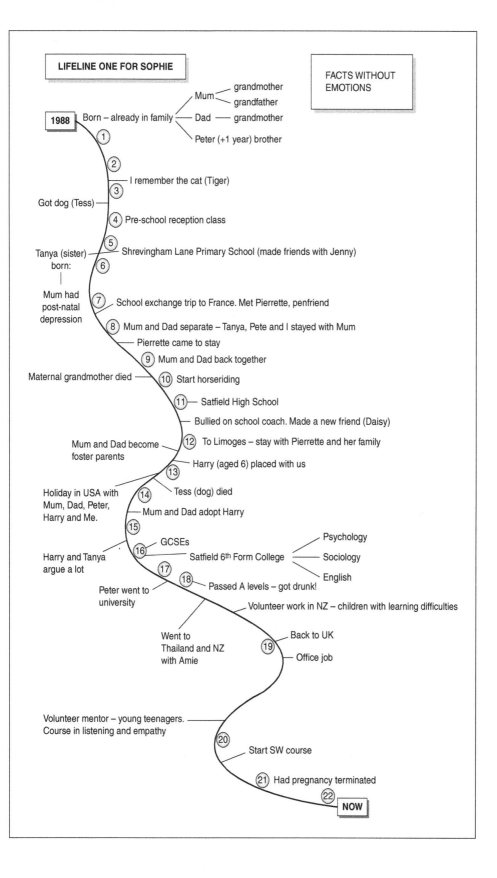

LIFELINE ONE FOR SOPHIE

FACTS WITHOUT EMOTIONS

1988

Born – already in family

- Mum — grandmother
  - grandfather
- Dad — grandmother
- Peter (+1 year) brother

① 

② 

③ I remember the cat (Tiger)

Got dog (Tess) —

④ Pre-school reception class

⑤ Shrevingham Lane Primary School (made friends with Jenny)

Tanya (sister) born:

⑥ 

Mum had post-natal depression

⑦ School exchange trip to France. Met Pierrette, penfriend

⑧ Mum and Dad separate – Tanya, Pete and I stayed with Mum

— Pierrette came to stay

⑨ Mum and Dad back together

Maternal grandmother died —⑩ Start horseriding

⑪— Satfield High School

— Bullied on school coach. Made a new friend (Daisy)

Mum and Dad become foster parents

⑫ To Limoges – stay with Pierrette and her family

— Harry (aged 6) placed with us

⑬ 

Holiday in USA with Mum, Dad, Peter, Harry and Me.

⑭ — Tess (dog) died

— Mum and Dad adopt Harry

⑮ 

— GCSEs

⑯ Satfield 6th Form College

- Psychology
- Sociology
- English

Harry and Tanya argue a lot

⑰ 

⑱ — Passed A levels – got drunk!

Peter went to university

— Volunteer work in NZ – children with learning difficulties

Went to Thailand and NZ with Amie

— Back to UK

⑲ 

— Office job

Volunteer mentor – young teenagers. Course in listening and empathy

⑳ 

— Start SW course

㉑ Had pregnancy terminated

㉒ NOW

*(Continued)*

- For example, if you are 24 years of age, and you started school when you were four years old, you should mark this in approximately one sixth of the way down the line.
- Keep writing in *facts*. For example, changes of school, moving house, family events such as holidays, illnesses in the family, becoming pregnant, new births, deaths, separations, divorces, marriages, passing or failing exams, starting college and so on.
- When you have done this retrace your steps and add further *factual* details. For example, can you write in the names of children and friends at your schools? Jot down their names, and those of your teachers too.
- Keep adding more factual detail as memories return to you.

Note that this is not a memory test. Rather, it is the beginning of a disciplined exercise in self-awareness. When you have finished writing in the facts keep your LIFELINE in a safe place, ready for the next stage in the exercise.

### Exercise 3(B): talking with a partner about your LIFELINE

When you have finished this first part of the exercise find a partner and take it in turns to talk one another through the 'facts' of your lives. Restrict your presentation to saying things like 'I was born in 1984' and resist any temptation to discuss feelings – they will come later.

### Exercise 3(C): remembering the feelings

- Now you turn to the third stage of the LIFELINE exercise in which you retrace your steps through the facts of your life but this time write in the *feelings* that are associated with the facts. For guidance, see LIFELINE 2 which is Sophie's factual LIFELINE with some emotions added.
- For example, a particular life event such as moving home when you were aged 10 might have caused you to feel *sad* at the loss of friends, or *excited* at the prospect of making new friends and starting at another school.
- Try to recall what these life events felt like *at the time they happened*, not what they feel like now, and write in the feelings alongside the event.
- Continue your way down the LIFELINE and spot life events that hold for you specific emotional memories and, in particular, note any life events about which emotions were mixed. For example, the break-up of a close relationship may bring with it a mixture of sadness and relief. Or the first few days at college may bring with them feelings of excitement mixed with anxiety.
- Other life events may cause distress – perhaps family illnesses or deaths.
- Are you able to see a time when you *defended yourself* from emotional pain?
- As you write in the emotions by the side of the life events you may find it helpful to use a different coloured pen so that they stand out.

As you work at remembering your feelings you may be helped by looking at the LIFELINE 2 diagram. In the example of Sophie she may, for example, be able to recall her feelings (aged four) when Tess (her dog) came to live with the family, or when she went to Limoges (aged seven) to stay with her penfriend, Pierrette.

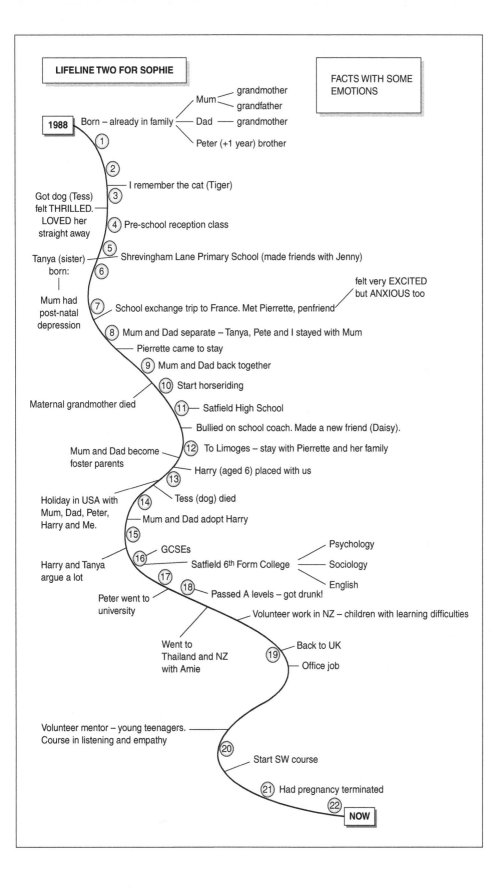

**LIFELINE TWO FOR SOPHIE**

**FACTS WITH SOME EMOTIONS**

1988 — Born – already in family

Mum — grandmother
— grandfather
Dad — grandmother
Peter (+1 year) brother

(1)

(2)
— I remember the cat (Tiger)

(3)
Got dog (Tess) felt THRILLED. LOVED her straight away

(4) Pre-school reception class

(5)
Shrevingham Lane Primary School (made friends with Jenny)

Tanya (sister) born:
|
Mum had post-natal depression

(6)

(7) School exchange trip to France. Met Pierrette, penfriend — felt very EXCITED but ANXIOUS too

(8) Mum and Dad separate – Tanya, Pete and I stayed with Mum
— Pierrette came to stay

(9) Mum and Dad back together

(10) Start horseriding

Maternal grandmother died

(11) — Satfield High School
— Bullied on school coach. Made a new friend (Daisy).

Mum and Dad become foster parents

(12) To Limoges – stay with Pierrette and her family
— Harry (aged 6) placed with us

(13)

Holiday in USA with Mum, Dad, Peter, Harry and Me.

(14) — Tess (dog) died
— Mum and Dad adopt Harry

(15)

Harry and Tanya argue a lot

(16) GCSEs
Satfield 6th Form College — Psychology
— Sociology
— English

(17)

(18) — Passed A levels – got drunk!

Peter went to university

— Volunteer work in NZ – children with learning difficulties

Went to Thailand and NZ with Amie

(19) — Back to UK
— Office job

Volunteer mentor – young teenagers. Course in listening and empathy

(20) Start SW course

(21) Had pregnancy terminated

(22) NOW

*(Continued)*

**Exercise 3(D): working on two tasks with a partner**

1 Pick one life event with its accompanying emotion(s), and describe it to your partner.
2 Try to identify, and tell your partner about, any past relationship or life event that has influenced your decision to become a social worker.
3 If you are the partner, carefully listen to the person you are partnered with and try not to interrupt or question them. Rather, try to empathise quietly with what they felt.
4 When you have finished, change roles with your partner.

**LIFELINE – the learning points**

- As with the genogram and many other exercises in this book, the purpose of the LIFELINE is to help you to increase your self-awareness.
- At this stage of the LIFELINE exercise you have begun to construct a document that shows the social and emotional influences there have been upon your life. It is these that have in large part shaped the person who you are today.
- You have also built upon the personal attachment map (Chapter 3) by tracking the facts and feelings of your relational history – both with family and friends.
- By talking through your LIFELINE with another person you have probably learned things about yourself.
- By listening carefully to facts and feelings in your partner's life you have built upon your empathy skills.
- Your learning about yourself is the same as learning about the main tool for use in relationship based social work.

When you have finished keep your LIFELINE in a safe place, ready to use it again.

## THE USE OF SELF

Throughout the chapter the phrase 'use of self' has been used, but it has been clear that before social workers can do this with competence they should know the 'self' that they are trying to use.

The deeper a person enters into self-knowledge the more able he or she is to think about and locate themselves within a state that is sometimes called the 'human condition'. This kind of location of the self means that not only is a person aware of his or her immediate life events and their accompanying emotions, but they are also able to position these events and feelings within a broader and deeper understanding of humanity.

For example, if someone with whom we are in a close relationship abruptly leaves us for another person the result for us is probably deep emotional pain and, perhaps, depression. But as (and if) the immediacy of the pain recedes we become more able to stand back from ourselves and think about what has happened in a different kind of a way. One of the most likely words to come into our mind is 'loss', for the experience brought with it the loss of a person, the loss of the role of being someone's partner, perhaps the loss of self-confidence...and so on.

The further away we are able to stand from the immediate experience, the easier it becomes for us to locate ourselves within the greater experience of being human. Our personal experience of loss is, in a more general sense and in its many forms, endemic to the human condition. The more we can reflect upon our own lives as individual examples of what it is to be human, the more able we are to place ourselves within a universalised sense of emotional constructs. We move ourselves on to a meta-level of being human, achieving a more intense experience of being a member of the human race.

Such a move changes us. Through it we deepen our personal humanity to the point where it is everyone's humanity. At this shared level our story resembles to some extent everyone's story. Of course the specifics are different, but what underlies it is what underlies the common human condition. And it is this move towards locating ourselves within the deep experience of being human that makes empathy a possibility. We become capable in our imaginations of feeling what it is like to be the other person. This is the place from where the self can be used in the relationship because, metaphorically speaking, one's self *is* the other person: we are bonded by a shared humanity.

It therefore seems that when we become more deeply ourselves then we are able to become more profoundly in touch with others. We *use* our life experiences to aid our understanding of and compassion with our client. It is this enhanced awareness of the self, leading to a deeper awareness of the other person, on which the use of self is based.

## CHAPTER SUMMARY

- This chapter has had an intrapersonal focus, emphasising the central part played by self-awareness in relationship based social work and the use of self.
- You have seen that self-awareness is linked to social work theory, values and skills.
- Through the genogram and LIFELINE exercises, and through work in pairs, you have had the opportunity to increase your awareness of the social, emotional and relational influences that have shaped the unique person that you are.
- Through case examples you have considered the benefits of self-awareness, but also the self-defensive obstructions that workers can (often unknowingly) put in its way.
- As your self-awareness increases, so you are more able to 'use' yourself in your professional practice, and locate your 'self' within a broader understanding of what it means to be human.
- This understanding can promote deeper levels of relationships.

*Further reading*

Ferguson, H. (2005) 'Working with violence, the emotions and the psycho-social dynamics of child protection: reflections on the Victoria Climbié case', *Social Work Education, 24, (7), October,* pp. 781–795.
This journal article reveals the ways in which workers might defend themselves from aspects of their work and thereby fail to engage fully with their clients and their behaviours.

Howe, D. (1998) 'Relationship-based thinking and practice in social work', *Journal of Social Work Practice, 2,(1).*
This seminal article argues that both a knowledge of human relationships, and being relational, lie at the heart of effective social work.

Winnicott, C. 'Development towards self-awareness' (2004) [1964] in Kanter, J. (2004).
This is another classic article in the history of relationship based social work. It is written from a psychodynamic perspective. The argument is that if social workers reduce their defences and become more self-aware they will, in so doing, enhance their awareness of their clients.

# 5 KNOWING THE OTHER PERSON IN RELATIONSHIP BASED SOCIAL WORK

## INTRODUCTION

Knowing ourselves appears to be the foundation for knowing other people (Howe 2008). And knowing other people, and other people knowing that we know them, provides them with the experience of being more deeply understood – perhaps more than ever before in their life. Such understanding creates the circumstances in which they can begin to *understand themselves* – why they feel, think and act as they do. And their growing self-awareness provides them with the best possibility of creating change in their lives, of experiencing an enhanced degree of constructive control over their human and material environments. This kind of therapeutic client-change is the heart of and rationale for relationship based practice.

In order to understand more about how this kind of social work can be achieved the chapter will explore the theory of emotional intelligence and the corresponding practice of empathy. Both help social workers to make sense of human situations and know the other person. Both optimise workers' chances of forming creative and co-operative professional relationships with their clients so that, in turn, clients may relate more creatively to themselves and to others.

With regard to practical skills, you will work on enhancing your emotional intelligence, your ability to listen to another person and empathise with what you hear. Communication, both verbal and non-verbal, will run as a thread throughout the chapter.

The content of the chapter relates to:

Key Role 1, Element 1.3 –

Develop a strategy to enable a purposeful relationship.

Key Role 2, Element 5.1 –

Provide emotional and practical support to:

- enable people to express, explore and assess their feelings and emotions.
- sustain people through the process of change.
- develop a supportive relationship.

## REASON AND EMOTION AS THE BASES FOR KNOWING THE OTHER PERSON

What is it that social workers require in order to 'know' or 'assess' another person? What tools do they need? Different social work agencies have different answers to these questions because often they will use a distinctive assessment tool that relates to the focused services that they provide. This means that the tool may be quite restricted in its scope because it will be attempting only to assess criteria such as 'need' or 'risk' in a particular area of a client's life. Specialist social workers and agencies require these specialist assessment tools but, in this chapter, the notion of 'knowing' and 'assessing' another person will be considered in a broader, more holistic way.

In the most general terms our ability to know another person is based on our ability to reason and to feel – both in relation to ourselves and the other person. It is the reasoning and the feeling dimensions of our mental lives, the cognitive and the emotional, that enable us to 'make sense' of what we perceive. In some situations we may make more use of what is cognitively known, and in other situations we may rely more upon what is felt but, in general, both of these areas of our mental processing are required for accurate assessment to be made.

In order to illustrate this, consider the following case study which describes an everyday transaction by a social worker in a children and families team.

 **Case Study One**

**Using reason and emotion in social work practice**

Carefully read the following description of a social work transaction in which you imagine yourself to be a social worker in a children and families team. You have on your caseload Polly, a six-year-old girl who is the subject of a Care Order. She lives with foster parents.

**Stage 1**

Polly's father has been released recently from a five-year prison term for his part in a robbery. He is angry because Polly's mother is living with another man, and because Polly's reception into care was on the grounds of emotional abuse. He wants to resume contact with Polly though he has not seen her since she made a prison visit three years ago. You discuss his request with your team manager and decide that any contact between Polly and her father must be supervised by the foster parents who have been trained in such work.

**Stage 2**

You check with the foster parents, ensuring that they agree to these arrangements, and you meet with Polly's father to discuss them with him. When you explain that the contact will be supervised he shows distress in his face but says nothing about how he feels. Instead he argues in a slightly raised voice that he should be allowed to take his daughter out on his own. However, he eventually concedes that he will see her under supervision in the foster home.

**Stage 3**

The following Sunday Polly's father goes to the foster home in accordance with the contact arrangements. Not long after his arrival an argument starts between him and the foster mother, and it escalates into a heated exchange with the foster father.

**Stage 4**

On Monday morning the foster mother contacts you to say that she and her husband feel uncertain about supervising any further contact. She says that Polly has refused to go to school and that last night she wet her bed – something that hasn't happened for months past.

---

**Practical work based on Case Study One (Done alone and with a partner)**

A) *Using your imagination,* make a written list of the emotions that you think may be present in Polly's father.

If you are not always sure what an emotion is, try putting the words 'I feel...' in front of it. For example, 'I feel *happy...*', 'I feel *worried...*'

In compiling your list of emotions use single words or phrases such as *frustrated, bitter, sad, let down, confused, angry...* and so on.

B) Having written down what you imagine Polly's father may be feeling, find a partner and compare your ideas. Try to tell your partner *why* you think he is feeling as he is. This will require you to *reason* about his emotional state, and link what you know of his life events to his feelings.

---

## ANALYSING THE SOCIAL WORK TRANSACTION WITH POLLY'S FATHER

When the transaction between Polly's father and the social worker is analysed it can be seen that part of it was a rational decision about a practical matter, and part was the emotional content of the decision.

The rational part concerns an agreement about the father–child contact being supervised. It is an example of task focused social work brought to bear on a specific circumstance and behaviour.

The emotional part concerns the feelings that Polly's father had about contact being supervised. In comparison with rationally based agreements, emotions are less amenable to boundaries. In this situation it could be guessed that as well as the father having feelings about the supervised contact there are in his mind feelings about Polly's mother, her new partner, the abuse and, perhaps, his imprisonment... and so on.

During the interview the social worker did not enquire about these feelings but chose to focus solely on the rationally known and defined task. The interview concluded with apparent agreement by the father.

The later heated exchange between the father and the foster father might, possibly, have been avoided if the social worker had picked up on the father's feelings during the interview, and given him the opportunity to express what lay behind the distress showing in his face and his slightly raised voice. Observing and taking notice of these subtle changes in Polly's father could have warned the social worker that, although there was *verbal* agreement to the contact arrangements, there was not *emotional* agreement.

If the social worker had invited the father to say what he felt then the style of social work would have moved away from a purely task focused interaction towards one that was more relationally based. It would have attempted to engage wholly with the father and the way he felt about the wider situation, rather than concentrate on the one-dimensional requirement to agree to certain arrangements. Instead of the transaction being *empathic*, sensitive to the inner, *unspoken* mind of the father, it was narrowly centred upon the outcome and 'rational' means of achieving it.

A general lesson to be drawn here is that sometimes (usually, in fact) *emotions influence outcomes* and sometimes they exercise complete control over outcomes – even when they are not expressed in words. In the case of Polly's father, what seems like a rational decision made through reasoned discussion concealed an emotionally charged state of mind. What appears to the social worker to be a practical and logical procedure may be felt by the recipient as threatening, hurtful or insensitive. Emotions such as these will demand expression and will often undermine social work objectives if they are not expressed in a 'safe' arena. If social workers are to approach their work holistically they must work with both reason and emotion (Howe and Hinings 1995). Rational discourse and decisions can be undermined if they are in conflict with strong but possibly unexpressed feelings.

Whenever social workers enter into a relationship with a client there will be emotions present in both people; perhaps they will feel interested, bored, anxious, fearful, contented. And when workers practise social work relationally, that is knowingly and purposefully using themselves in a relationship, emotions become one of the key indicators of what is 'happening' in the transaction between them and their client. Emotions can impart information to social workers and guide them, but only if they are able to access them, name them, interpret and manage them. These are some of the marks of emotional intelligence.

## USING EMOTIONAL INTELLIGENCE IN SOCIAL WORK PRACTICE

In the case of Polly the social worker might have avoided the difficulties surrounding the father–daughter contact had she used her emotional intelligence. As it was, her practice tended towards being one-dimensional. It is an example of what Blaug (1995) calls 'instrumentalism' – in this instance, using the encounter only for the delivery of a decision to a person and not as a sensitive engagement with a man who is probably experiencing complex and conflicting feelings.

One-dimensional or instrumental social work is reason-based, and this is both a strength and a restriction. The strength is that social work must retain rationality if it is to operate from a disciplined and bureaucratically organised base that is designed to act decisively and efficiently where children, the mentally ill or the elderly and infirm need support and protection. But this reasoned strength can become a restriction on good practice if social workers over-rely on rationality in their assessments of human affairs.

A meeting such as that with Polly's father requires a multi-dimensional sensitivity on the part of the worker: being aware of the less definable subtleties of feelings that surround the core business of making contact arrangements. How can the concept of emotional intelligence help workers to construct a multi-dimensional social work practice that can engage with these often invisible subtleties? It is to this concept that we now turn, first examining it in a general way and then specifically in relation to social work.

### Mayer and Salovey

Among the pioneers of the concept of emotional intelligence are Salovey and Mayer (1990). In that early publication they defined it as 'the ability to monitor one's own and others' feelings and emotions, to discriminate among them and to use this information to guide one's thinking and actions'. Although ideas about emotional intelligence have been developed since Salovey and Mayer first wrote, these concepts of self-awareness and other-awareness have remained at the core.

In more recent work Mayer, Salovey and Caruso (2000) set out their Four Branch model of emotional intelligence.

## The four branch model of emotional intelligence

1 The *perceiving* branch which includes the *perception, appraisal* and *expression* of emotion. Key here is the ability to *recognise emotions in other people* (such as Polly's father's use of non-verbal communication) and those within the self (again, perhaps by physical states such as heart beating or sweating). It also includes the ability to express emotions in ways that are constructive.
2 The *facilitating* branch concerns our ability to *use emotions* as an aid to thinking, to understand how emotions can direct us towards information that we need, helping us to prioritise thoughts and engage with multiple viewpoints.
3 The *understanding* branch helps us to *analyse what we and others are feeling.* We develop a vocabulary of emotions and understand the links between them and experience (e.g. 'happiness' might be associated with passing an exam). We also understand that emotions can exist in complex mixtures (e.g. love and hate together) and that emotions are often in 'transition' (e.g. anger turns into guilt about being angry).
4 The *managing* branch is the ability to *stay open to feelings that are pleasant and unpleasant.* The person who can manage feelings is able to reflect upon or detach from an emotion, depending upon how informative or useful it is. They are able to judge their emotions, how typical they are in terms of their normality, how influential they are (e.g. over decision making) and how reasonable (e.g. fair or unfair) they are to others. Finally, the person who can manage their emotions is more likely to be able to use them as sources of personal, intellectual or emotional growth. (adapted from Maltby et al. 2007: 368–369)

In summary, emotional intelligence describes the ability to *recognise* the presence of emotions in ourselves and others. This recognition helps us to *express* emotions in ways that are constructive, and to *use* them as an aid to our thinking and our perceiving of others' views. It helps us to *understand* why we or others are feeling as we do, and this understanding helps us to *manage* our feelings, not rushing to suppress unpleasant ones but remaining open to learning what they can tell us.

The power and the utility of the concept of emotional intelligence lies in its description of human life that we can all recognise – for each of us has experienced situations where emotional intelligence has been present or absent – and it is that which has made all the difference to what has happened next. In the model the authors have succeeded in conceptualising and encapsulating what, for many people, is a normal way of relating to themselves and to other people. Most people are, to an extent, routinely aware of their feelings, and they are sensitive to the feelings of others. In general, people dislike the thought of 'hurting' another person's feelings, and would seek to make amends if they did. We are also able to associate feelings with events and, if we reflect on our life experiences, we know that some behaviours can cause us to feel 'bitter sweet'; that is, to have mixed feelings such as guilt and pleasure. And, again, many people for much of the time are sufficiently able to manage their feelings – to reason about them and achieve a balance for themselves and others. When this does not happen it is often the hard to manage feelings such as extreme anger, guilt, rage or jealousy that 'spill over' and, taking no account of reason, result in emotionally driven behaviour that can harm both one-self and others.

The concept of emotional intelligence brings together into one framework what is the best of balanced human behaviour: in the mind and, by extension, by the body. It requires us to understand others and ourselves holistically, multi-dimensionally, and understanding at this level will lead towards personal, intellectual and emotional growth. This is true for all human beings, but social workers' professional calling places upon them an enhanced responsibility to know, intelligently manage and use their emotions so that, when brought face to face with the emotional states of their clients, they may respond in a constructive, reasoned, 'sense-making' and emotionally sensitive manner.

The following case study focuses upon an example of social work practice where emotions are to the fore. As you read it concentrate on the *emotional* content of the information. It is divided into four stages that in part relate to the Four Branch model of emotional intelligence.

---

 **Case Study Two**

**Using emotional intelligence in everyday social work**

Carefully read the following description of a social work transaction in which you imagine yourself to be a social worker in an inner city adult services team that operates a 'drop in' service.

**Stage 1**

You are on duty, and the team receptionist calls you to see a young woman who is not previously known to you. She has with her two children who you later learn are aged two and three. The first thing that you notice about the woman is that her left cheek is bruised. You enquire why she has come to adult services and she explains that, the night before, her male partner had punched her body and face. You ask her if this has happened before and she tells you that it has never been so bad, but that he has hit her before. As she gives her account of the relationship you notice that she twists the rings on her fingers and that she is patient with the three-year-old who is persistent in asking her to look at the toy he has found in the interviewing room. You feel some admiration for this woman's apparent ability to carry on in the face of adversity. But you also feel a stirring of anger within yourself that she has to.

**Stage 2**

It registers in your mind that your client is in an anxious state – and you, too, start to feel the mild anxiety that sometimes comes when we do not know what is going to be said next. You bring your own anxiety into your awareness, and then you continue the interview by gently asking her to tell you more about her partner. The man

*(Continued)*

*(Continued)*

who has been violent is the father of the 2-year-old, but the older child has another father. Your client acknowledges that she no longer loves her partner, and that friends say she is wrong to stay with him. You say that you are wondering if she may feel a bit frightened to leave, and that staying may seem preferable to being alone? As you say this your relationship with your partner passes through your mind, and you deliberately bring your focus back to your client. She doesn't respond to what you have said but you notice that she seems to be trying not to cry. You feel surprised when she says that she has got to go. She calls the children, and leaves the room. You return to your office and discuss with your manager the oft-found linkages between partner abuse and child abuse, and together you decide that further consideration must be given to the safeguarding implications for the children and their mother.

### Stage 3

Now you ponder what has happened. Why did she leave? Was it because of what you said? You do not know. You ask yourself if, for some people, it's better to be in a violent relationship than in no relationship. If a person suffers from basic anxiety, and has a dread of being abandoned, might they feel that it is worth paying the cost of staying with a person who other people would regard as destructive and offering no positive future? If a person has a fragile belief in their ability to cope alone is the thought of doing so too anxiety provoking? These questions circulate in your mind. You think of attachment theory and its analysis of insecurities. You think of psychoanalytic theory and the ways in which a victim may believe irrationally that her punishment must be deserved. You think of behavioural theory and how victims may have learned to blame themselves for the violent acts of others. You reflect that human behaviours, and the emotions that they generate, can mean quite different things to different people. As you think through these things you shudder at the thought of a partner being violent with you.

### Stage 4

Later that day, at home, the case returns to your mind. Your pondering on your client's feelings has given way to experiencing your own. You feel frustrated, and a little angry with this person, and you wonder why. In trying to understand yourself you realise that, while listening to your client, you already had in your mind the idea that she and the children should leave this violent man and move into the women's refuge. Your frustration is associated with the client leaving the office abruptly, before you could make this suggestion. And your anger with her is connected with her being, and seemingly choosing to remain, a victim. It surprises you that you feel more angry with her than with her violent partner. But the more that you are able to stand back from your feelings the more unreasonable they seem. This client has the right to live her life and make her own decisions. You are not entitled to impose a solution on her.

### Practical work based on Case Study Two

With your partner work through the four stages in the case study and relate each one to the corresponding branch in the Four Branch model of emotional intelligence.

- Where can you detect this social worker using her emotional intelligence?
- Are there times when *more* emotional intelligence could have been shown?
- Something about the service user seemed to resonate with the social worker's personal life, though you are not told exactly what it was. What is the 'emotionally intelligent' way of managing this kind of unexpected linkage between oneself and a service user? (Note: more will be said about this in Chapter 6).

Discuss these questions with your class partner.

## Learning from the case study

Emotional intelligence offers social work a framework of linked ideas which it can use to analyse separate parts of the emotional processes at work within and between people. The social worker in the above case demonstrated her ability to *perceive*, to notice her client's behaviours (the non-verbal communication of ring-twisting, the apparent patience with the child), and also to notice the emotional effects that her client, and the account of the violence, were having on her (feeling admiration for her client, but mild anger too). This ability in the social worker to be aware of both herself and the other person is an indication that the worker was psychologically as well as physically present in the encounter – an essential foundation of relationship based practice.

In stage 2, that of *facilitating* emotions, the social worker (probably with accuracy) perceived that her client was anxious. She also noticed her own mild anxiety and perhaps her mind registered that anxiety is sometimes 'catching': if one person in a close encounter is feeling it, then a similar feeling might be activated in the other. The client is beginning to impart information (she no longer loves her partner, friends say she should leave) but then comes a pivotal point in the interview. The social worker, rather than letting the client's emotions give direction to the encounter, attempts to *analyse* the service user's behaviour. She asks her client, albeit in a gentle manner, if she is frightened to leave her violent partner. While we should not be over-critical of the intervention, for it might have been empathic and correct, its timing appears to have been counter-productive, and the client brings the interview to an abrupt end. It is an example of what some therapists call 'pushing the client's river' instead of letting it flow freely.

Stage 3, *understanding* emotions and how certain feelings come to be associated with certain life experiences, is well illustrated in the case study. The worker understands that emotions are complex and that they do not follow what may appear to be a rational course of action (e.g. leave violent relationships). It was the worker's enhanced level of understanding that informed her verbal intervention, although it was apparently mistimed.

Stage 4, *managing* emotions is illustrated by the social worker's reflective period later in the day. She strives to understand why she feels as she does, and perhaps she ponders how she could have conducted the interview in a more constructive way, and one that would have led to another outcome. This worker engages in the kind of reflective practice that is a hallmark of emotional intelligence.

## EMOTIONS, OUTCOMES, AND THE WORKER'S TASK OF 'HOLDING' THE SITUATION

This case study in the use of emotional intelligence (like that of Polly and her father) describes a situation where emotions appear to have determined the outcome. What a client feels in a situation such as this is likely to override all rational analysis. Of course, this is not to say that rational analysis has no place, but it is to say that it should be kept in its place, which is usually *after* strong emotions have been expressed and a degree of catharsis has been facilitated.

Metaphorically speaking, emotions can fly all over the place. They can be acted out in shouting, erratic and unpredictable behaviours, but unless these are extreme or dangerous they are to be held within the social worker/client relationship. This is the space within which things can be said and felt, yet contained – and such saying and feeling will usually and eventually evolve into a situation where things can be thought through. Reason follows on from emotion if (and sometimes only if) the worker–client relationship is there as a facilitative and holding environment.

This kind of social work is mirroring the relationship between carer and child that was explored in Chapter 3. There it was seen that the formation of the child was critically altered by the kind of relationships he or she experienced with the care-giving adults. Good carers hold their child's emotions, helping them to manage them and feel safe while experiencing them. Carers who are not so good at their task may be unable to provide such holding. Whatever experiences a child has had, or not had, in terms of being held emotionally, are likely to be transferred into some situations in adult life. For example, a child who sought comfort and attention in infancy, but met with rebuttal, may transfer the feeling of 'rejection' in childhood on to help-seeking situations in adulthood. While it is too simplistic to say that the situations of childhood and adulthood will feel identical, it is nevertheless likely that they will resonate in some way – probably unconsciously – within the person's emotional mind. For we carry hurts within us and early rejections may lead to the expectation of rejections in later life. And such expectations may lead to defensive and, possibly, aggressive behaviours. In order to engage creatively and meaningfully with such behaviours the social worker needs her emotional intelligence – her enhanced ability to perceive, facilitate, understand and manage her behavioural repertoire and the effects that her clients' emotional and physical behaviours have upon her.

## PRACTISING EMOTIONAL INTELLIGENCE

Once the concept of emotional intelligence is understood it is developed within the self by practising it. It is to your practice that we now turn.

### Exercise One

### The guided walk (Done with a partner)

This is an exercise done in pairs, one person being guided and the other acting as guide. It is more interesting, and learning is enhanced, if the pairs go out of the classroom to explore the building and outside the building too.

The exercise works best if the guided person is blindfolded by a scarf – for then they truly rely on their guide. The work of the guide is primarily to keep their partner safe from danger so, as the guide, you will usually be holding your partner's arm, and giving them verbal warnings of approaching hazards such as doorways or steps. But the guide should also attempt to bring interest to the walk. For example, suggest that the guided person touches things such as a leaf on a tree or the texture of concrete (it is astonishing how acute the sense of touch becomes when it is not accompanied by sight); tell them about their surroundings and the things that they cannot see. Perhaps take them in a lift. Again, the sensation of ascending or descending becomes exaggerated throughout the body when sight is absent (in a normally sighted person).

The group might contain students who are visually impaired. They will decide the level at which they want to join in the exercise. Depending on their level of sight impairment they may have helpful comments to make about relying on and trusting others to guide them.

### The purposes of the exercise

The exercise has two purposes; one for the guide and one for the guided.

The guide should try to perceive and understand his 'client's' state of mind. In this exercise it is usual for a normally sighted person to experience some anxiety, but also pleasurable excitement mixed with caution and, perhaps, distrust in the ability of their guide to keep them safe. The guide should also try to become aware of his own feelings – perhaps of the great responsibility he has for protecting the person whom he is guiding.

The guided person should try to be aware of and name (to themselves) their feelings *as they are experienced*. Try to bring an immediacy into your self-awareness. For example, if you move from inside a building to outside, you are likely to notice a change in temperature. First let this enter experience and then, if you can, find a word to describe it.

### Stage 1

The walk should last between five and 10 minutes. When it is finished, swap roles.

### Stage 2

Back in the classroom, stay with your partner and exchange your feelings about the experience.

In particular, the guide should say what he imagined the 'client's' feelings to be at different times, and the client should say what it actually felt like. How well do these versions about the emotional impact of the experience correspond with each other?

The guided walk exercise mirrors *emotionally* many social worker/client transactions insofar as a client is often vulnerable, and relying on the worker to do carefully what is in their best interests.

As the *guided*, it may be that you are like an apprehensive child coming into care under an Emergency Protection Order, or an anxious adult being taken against your will to the psychiatric hospital. Or your need of your guide could resemble the need felt by an older person for the familiar face of their social worker as they leave their home for the last time in order to enter residential care. Being guided gets you in touch with your reactions towards trusting (or not) another human being. You may have sensed your vulnerability and, in so doing, have come into contact with a feeling that is often present in clients of social workers. In this way the exercise puts you in emotional touch with the 'client' within yourself.

As the *guide* you are like a social worker managing the practical aspects of a physical journey that your client is making. But you are also managing the emotional dimensions – the *meaning* and *experience* of the journey. Sometimes you will be the holder of your client's emotions, their safe container. In your person you may become for them a symbolic and safe 'object' whose presence allows them to contain themselves. At times such as these you are practising in a relational manner with your client, and your relationship is informed by a deep awareness of their feelings and their needs.

---

**Exercise Two**

**Life events and their emotions**

The word 'emotion' carries the idea of energy or power. Emotions are thus called because they put us into motion, and common phrases such as being *moved to tears* convey the dynamic effects between event and feeling. We may also be swayed, carried away, swept up, consumed or controlled by emotion. We, and our perceptions of things around us, are not the same after we have experienced emotion.

Certain emotions can exercise a particularly strong and lasting hold on us. Some, such as anger, jealousy, hatred or sadness, may become life-diminishing, especially if they persist through time. Others, such as love that is returned or joy at the arrival of spring sunshine, can be exciting, anticipatory and life-enhancing.

In the following exercise you return to the personal LIFELINE that you began to construct when you read the last chapter. You are asked to look again at events in your life and select *one* that has an association with feelings of *loss*, or *vulnerability* or *anxiety* (there are some ideas to help you with this in the Stage 1 box below). Sometimes the exercise is made more effective by bringing into the class photographs of yourself or others that date from the time of the life event.

This exercise is in four stages. In Stage 3 you will either be telling a partner about your life event, or listening to the life event of your partner. When you are the listener your learning (and your partner's) will be enhanced if you follow this simple and practical guide to good communication that is adapted from Egan (1977: 114). It can be memorised through the letters S–O–L–E–R.

**S** = sit facing the other person – in body language it says 'I am with you'.

**O** = adopt an open posture (e.g. don't fold your arms over your chest because it might convey to the other person that you are closing yourself off).

**L** = lean slightly towards the person sometimes (you'll probably do this without thinking about it as a sign of interest and involvement).

**E** = is for eye contact – try to make it. Think of eyes as windows into the mind of the other person.

**R** = try to relax – with the person, even if you cannot relax with what they are saying.

Like all experiential learning, doing these kinds of things may at first seem contrived and, perhaps, embarrassing. But persist with them and in time you will feel the benefits.

---

## Stage 1

### Choosing a life event (Done on your own)

You have already begun to write in the emotions that were connected with some of your life events. Now focus in particular on an experience that provoked the feeling of *vulnerability* or *loss* or *anxiety* in your life.

This experience does not need to be extraordinary. It is the ordinary and everyday kind of life event that may best help you to work at enhancing your emotional intelligence. Pick an event that involved other people as well as yourself. Examples could be:

- leaving a school where you had made good friends;
- being bullied;
- witnessing an argument between your parents;
- getting into trouble at school;
- someone close being ill;
- an argument with your mum about staying out late;
- feeling certain that you have failed an exam;
- feeling sure that one day your boyfriend or girlfriend will leave you;
- a pet dying;
- the break-up of your first serious relationship.

Remember that although feelings of loss are usually associated with losing a thing or a person, they often lead on to less tangible losses such as the loss of self-confidence, or self-esteem. In the extreme they can be the basis of depression.

Vulnerability might be a response to a visible and physical threat (such as bullying), or it might be associated with a more subtle and invisible experience such as rejection by a person from whom you want love. Vulnerability is associated with feeling uncertain, afraid or out of control.

Similarly, anxiety is associated with something unpleasant that you believe may happen in the future. It can be 'rational' (i.e. you have good reason to believe it will happen) or 'irrational' (where you have no evidence for your belief).

As you undertake this exercise you may be helped by referring back to the LIFELINE of Sophie, the imaginary social work student, and see how she might select a life event that led to feelings of loss, anxiety or vulnerability (LIFELINE 3). Perhaps the most obvious ones are when her parents separated, or when her pregnancy was terminated, but do not overlook life events that are less obviously associated with loss or anxiety but may, nevertheless, provoke these feelings. In Sophie's case an event such as Harry (foster child) coming to live with the family may have created anxiety, as well as excitement.

---

### Stage 2

**Your life event, the emotions, and your emotional intelligence (Done on your own)**

When you have chosen a life event, write down the emotions that were associated with it. Do this systematically, in the following stages:

1 Briefly describe the event. It might be helpful to include what you understand to have been the immediate cause, and what followed on from it. In other words, put the event in context.
2 Write down a description of your own emotions – noting in particular mixed emotions (for example sadness and relief). Note also if your emotions changed through time.
3 Write down what you imagine to have been the emotions of the other people involved. Do not analyse the situation in a logical way. Rather, just try to engage empathically with others' feelings (which may seem to be in tension, e.g. a parent who feels both love and anger).
4 Now assess your emotional intelligence by attempting to answer these questions:

   (a) How well, at the time, did you perceive and understand other people's emotions?
   (b) How well did you manage the effects of their emotions on you?
   (c) How well did you understand and manage your own emotions?

### Stage 3

**Describing your life event (Done with a partner)**

When you have completed Stage 2 find a partner to work with. Your task is to:

1 describe the life event;
2 describe your emotions;
3 describe what you think other people's emotions were.

*The role of the partner*

As the partner, using SOLER, your role is to *listen* attentively, ask few or no questions, and practise being emotionally intelligent about your class partner's description of their life event. Try to empathise with their emotional position. That is, put out of your mind any thoughts about what they or others should or should not have done, or any brilliant ideas you have about better solutions to what you are hearing.

---

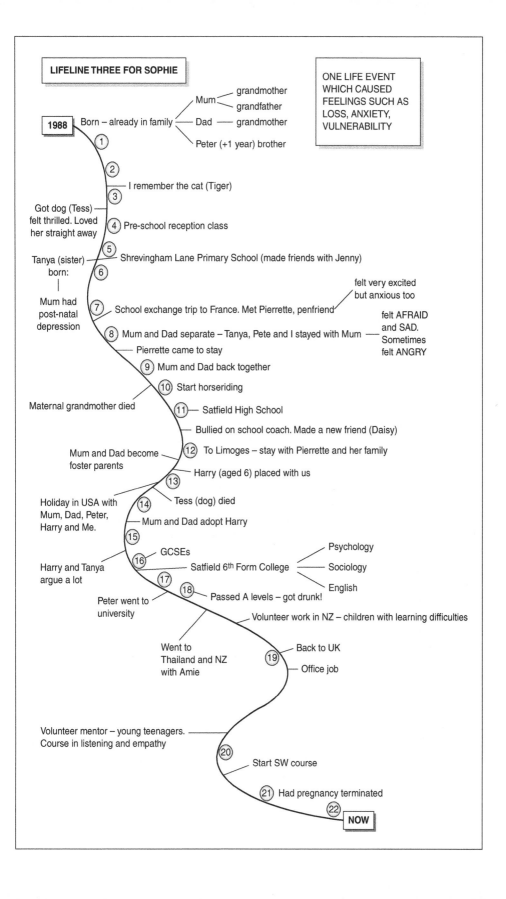

*(Continued)*

Instead, just try to focus on what *they* felt at the time, and resist any urge to judge whether it was right or wrong, wise or unwise, and so on.

**Stage 4**

**Reflection and evaluation**

Now is the time to reflect together on the exercise. Look again at the Four Branch model of emotional intelligence and use each part – perceiving, facilitating, understanding and managing emotion – to evaluate the life event and the emotions that were felt by the actors involved. Try to say how emotionally intelligent you think you were *at the time*. Did you *really* know what you were feeling, why you were feeling it, what others were feeling? Were some people emotionally intelligent and others not? Were some driven along by emotional forces that they did not seem to understand and could not control?

Now the partners change places and the listener describes an event in his or her life.

*A note of caution …*

Sometimes an exercise like this can stir up unwelcome memories and you may need some further time, perhaps spent with a friend, to reflect on this experience in your life.

In this exercise you have had the opportunity to gain increased awareness of your own emotional experience, and the effects it has had on you, and you have listened attentively to the emotional experience of your class partner. The exercise is designed to help you to practise recognising and understanding emotions in yourself and others, and to listen empathically to someone else's 'story'.

Emotional intelligence is a most important tool of relationship based practice. It provides a conceptual framework for understanding the importance of recognising that what your client is feeling will have an impact on the social work outcome. It will help you to facilitate the emotions of the other person, knowing that if they are brought to the surface of consciousness they can be worked with more creatively and, sometimes, used as a source of energy for constructive change. Even emotions that are hard to work with, such as a client's persisting anger, contain high levels of energy that may, perhaps, be channelled into creative uses by the skilled relationship based social worker.

Emotional intelligence also helps social workers to understand why someone is feeling as they are. They will be able to link this knowledge with their studies of human growth and behaviour, their knowledge that past life experiences colour and affect the present time. Their emotional intelligence will also assist them in linking their client's feelings with mental states that might border on mental illness – the obsessions, the paranoias and the delusions that can occupy people's minds and control their behaviours. And finally, emotional intelligence helps workers in the management of emotions – both their own and their client's. They may develop the skills of channelling emotions in directions that are more constructive. As Howe (2008: 195) writes, 'If we can be intelligent *about* emotions – what they are, why we have them, how they affect us – we can be more intelligent *with* them'.

Our intelligence must use both our reason and our emotion. Social workers should reason about what they and their clients feel, and feel about their reasoning. They might say to themselves, 'Does removing this child feel right?' – and behind such a question there may exist an intuitive feeling that it may not be right. In this kind of way reason and emotion inform and affect one another. They balance one another and together form the basis of holistic social work practice.

Emotional intelligence provides a theory and a practice model for relationship based social work. At its foundation is careful, attentive listening, and listening in this way leads us to empathy. Empathy is a route, perhaps *the* route, into being a practitioner who is skilled at knowing other people.

## EMPATHY AND LISTENING

You are not alone if you are not sure what empathy means. It is a state of mind that is difficult to define, and still more difficult to achieve in practice. Like self-awareness it is best to see it as a mental condition towards which we can tend. In other words, it may be achieved partially, but 'perfect' empathy is probably impossible to define or obtain.

Empathy is a way of 'hearing' what another person is 'saying', both verbally and non-verbally, at the emotional level. It is a way of practising social work that requires the worker to offer their own self in relationship, for it is only by opening themselves up in this way that they permit their client's feelings to enter into their own consciousness. Temporarily, and for a specific purpose, the worker's 'inner world' is in contact with the 'inner world' of the client. In this position the social worker would no longer be just a technician 'sorting out' human affairs. Rather, he or she would go deeper than that, engaging in the often unspoken *meanings* of these affairs for those most affected by them. Social work that understands people's viewpoints (though not always agreeing with them) leads to a more compassionate and effective practice. It is an emotionally intelligent practice that facilitates, where possible, co-operative and creative work with clients. Even in situations of discord or conflict, if workers can demonstrate that they 'know' and 'understand' their clients, then the chances of a constructive engagement are maximised.

But this empathic entry into the perceptual life of the other person does not mean losing sight of your own world, your professional duty to assess and act. Rather, and this is a key skill of relational practice, it means being in touch with yourself (as a professional with safeguarding responsibilities and a person with feelings) while, *at the same time,* engaging with the feelings of the other person. Wilson et al. (2008: 8) describe the skill as one of 'being able to simultaneously focus in professional encounters on what is happening for the service user and what is happening to you'. This simultaneous awareness of self and other is crucial if workers are to retain the *objectivity* required for critical tasks such as risk assessment while, at the same time, engaging *inter-subjectively* with their client. The following example demonstrates the objectivity of medical diagnosis and the subjectivity of mind-to-mind engagement.

---

**An example of empathy**

Imagine that you are very worried about some pains that you have and when you see your GP your worry has grown into a state of anxiety. Most of all in this situation you want your GP to be competent, knowing her job, but you also want her to do her job in a particular way. You want her to display compassionate understanding of your state of mind. If she has this compassion then she is likely to treat you sensitively, lovingly, while still competently performing her main task, which is to diagnose and treat what is wrong. If you are on the receiving end of a response like this then you are likely to feel that you have experienced empathy from another person.

---

## DISTINGUISHING EMPATHY FROM OTHER WAYS OF FEELING

The suffix 'pathy' means *feeling*, and when a prefix is attached a type or way of feeling is described. Three examples are *a*pathy, *sym*pathy and *em*pathy and, in order to understand further the meaning of empathy it is helpful to compare it with these other words.

When we talk of apathy, taken literally we mean 'no feeling'. The first part of Figure 5.1 displays two people who are making no contact with one another. If this lack of contact is deliberate we might say that these people are showing '*anti*pathy', whereas apathy is descriptive of a lack of emotion and interest.

The word 'sympathy' is quite different. The prefix 'sym' means 'with' (or sometimes 'united' or 'together') – and sympathy therefore means sharing feelings with another person. Sympathy between friends brings an emotional understanding and bond but in a social worker/client relationship it runs the danger of the worker becoming over-involved with the client, thereby ceasing to retain objectivity and the proper distance that is required for social work assessment. In the figure sympathy is pictured as two people emotionally immersed to the point where they are 'at one' with each other.

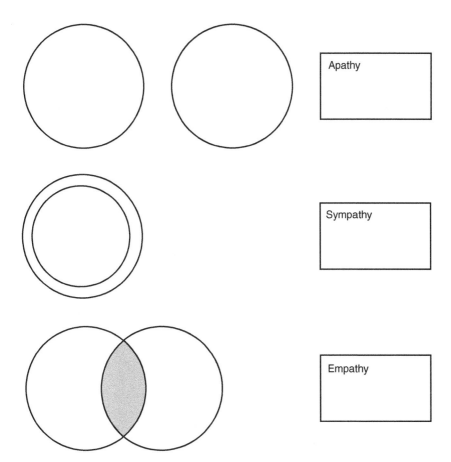

**Figure 5.1**

Empathy is different again. It is important to relationship based social work (and emotional intelligence) because it is the method through which the worker may make deeper contact with the emotional state of the client while avoiding over-immersion and the risk of losing objectivity. It is what Wilson et al. (2008) mean by focusing on the self *and* the other person. In the figure it is represented as the emotional worlds of the social worker and the client overlapping but, at the same time, a large part of the worker's self-awareness remains separate. Thus, being empathic means that the worker never loses sight of who they are personally, and who they are professionally in terms of their status and responsibilities.

A practical example of empathy might be when a social worker from a children and families team, through careful listening to a single parent, obtains a deep understanding of the reasons why the parent persistently neglects to feed and dress her child adequately and ensure that he gets to school. If this understanding is empathic (rather than sympathetic) the social worker will never take her eye off her primary concern, which is the child's well-being. Her response is empathic because it is entering into the inner world of the mother while, *at the same time*, she is retaining her sense of self as a worker in a child protection team. This balance comes with professional experience, but it is maintained through *supervision* and *personal reflection* (subjects for Chapter 6).

While this kind of empathic social work, carried out in a statutory and potentially high-risk situation, is different to the imaginary consultation with the GP, it bears some resemblance at a fundamental level. Like your GP, you are displaying empathic understanding and, through it, you may be able to detect in this single mother the unspoken presence of a despair and depression that underlie the neglect of her child. In doing this, you are using your emotional intelligence in the relationship. You are, in Howe's words, seeking to

> *understand* what is happening to people rather than discipline them into responsibility and good behaviour. When working with people it is better to *make sense* than to *impose* order. Interpretation is better than legislation. (2008: 194, emphasis in original)

Sense making in the way that Howe means requires a relationship in which some level of trust has been built up between worker and client. If and when the client feels understood by the worker, and experiences from the worker compassionate tolerance and practical assistance, then their behaviour (such as child neglect) is more likely to change. Of course, social workers are sometimes obliged to 'impose order' by removing a child but, if circumstances permit, the relationship based social worker would first try to 'understand' the inner worlds of those most involved for, through such understanding, statutory actions may be avoided.

## EMPATHY AND THE USE OF WORDS

Gerhardt (2004b: 205) writes of the developing child that 'at the earliest stage of life, safety and acceptance are conveyed by touch', but she adds that 'as we mature, we increasingly use words to "hold" each other'. Silent listening is an important part of an empathic response, but so are words. If the listener is able to 'give' words to a person, then they facilitate the person's ability to describe their inner world. Words are a way of accessing and externalising the hitherto unspoken and invisible inner self. They make available to another person what has been kept inside.

Empathy can also take the form of verbal questioning, or enquiry. For example, a relationship based social worker who senses anxiety in a 22-year-old woman who has received a diagnosis of possible schizophrenia, might gently enquire of her client, 'I wonder if you are feeling less sure about the future now you've heard this news...?'

The question might resonate with the client's inner though unspoken fears and, if it does, it may facilitate her in speaking about them. Of course, attempts at empathy such as this might be ineffective if they are inaccurate. Perhaps this client does not feel 'unsure', or maybe she is protecting herself from feelings such as these and therefore denies their existence. In such a case it is unlikely that any harm will be done, and sometimes inaccurate or untimely empathy can stimulate a client into eventually finding the right words for themselves.

Thus, an essential tool for the empathic worker is vocabulary. The English language abounds with 'feeling' words and the following exercise will help you to build up a stock of them.

---

**Exercise Three**

**Using language to assist empathy**

The exercise can be done by 'brainstorming' in the whole class, in small groups, or alone. It requires you to think of words that complete the sentence beginning 'perhaps you feel...'

To start you off, here is a list of feelings generated by a group of social work students in about 60 seconds:

| | | | | | |
|---|---|---|---|---|---|
| embarrassed | protective | upset | angry | deflated | frustrated |
| disliked | amused | happy | scared | shocked | helpless |
| empty | pity | pitied | sad | frightened | seething |
| uncomfortable | boiling | not bothered | overwhelmed | elated | |
| low | ashamed | horrible | horrified | disgusted | |

You may find it easier to go through the alphabet. Here are some examples starting with 'A':

| | | | | | |
|---|---|---|---|---|---|
| abandoned | abused | abased | abysmal | able | accountable |
| abhorrent | accused | abject | absolved | apathetic | |

If you brainstorm these in your groups you may be surprised at how many words you can think of that will be of practical use to you in knowing your clients. And, of course, if your clients feel that you know them, then they are more likely to respond constructively to your work.

---

## THE QUALITY OF EMPATHY

For social workers, increasing their vocabulary of emotions is one of the most basic and practical skills required for empathising with service users. But what of the theory of empathy? It was Carl Rogers more than any other person who put the word on the map of the helping professions.

Rogers was a contemporary of Maslow and, like him, he argued that inherent in the human condition is the urge to 'self-actualise' or 'reach one's potential'. His most lasting contribution to this way of thinking was in naming and analysing the *core relationship conditions* that facilitate such self-actualising development. These were empathy, warmth (sometimes called unconditional positive regard) and genuineness (sometimes called congruence).

He understood empathy as being in a state of mind that feels what another person is feeling and communicating this feeling in verbal and non-verbal ways. To relate in this way to another person, without making judgements about whether the feelings are right or wrong, is in itself a healing process. More than any other major theorist of this period (1950s–1970s), Rogers moved away from the analytical legacy of Freud. He argued that 'brilliance and diagnostic perceptiveness are unrelated to empathy' (1980 [1963]: 149) and claimed that empathy on its own '*is clearly related to positive outcome*' (1980: 150, his emphasis).

Rogers' claims for empathy have never been seriously challenged and as a theoretical concept and method of professional practice it has found its way into the mainstream of therapies that lie outside of his own, person-centred tradition. For example, Kohut (1977), coming from a post-Freudian psychoanalytical background, called empathy our 'psychological oxygen' and wrote that 'man can no more survive psychologically in a psychological milieu that does not respond empathically to him, than he can survive physically in an atmosphere that contains no oxygen' (Kohut 1977, quoted in Mischel et al. 2004: 131). For Kohut, empathy is the quality that allows parents to mirror back uncritically to their child how they see and experience him or her. Through this mirroring the child can grow in self-awareness and learn to connect together thoughts, behaviours and feelings. In this way the child's personal cohesion, his or her integrated identity is formed (see discussion in Becker 1992). In Kohut's analysis we can see links with a parent helping their child to develop emotional intelligence.

Such ideas about empathy echo and verify Rogers' claim (1980) that empathy is one of the core qualities that facilitates self-understanding, self-confidence, the ability to choose behaviours, the freedom to 'be and become'. He saw this way of being as tapping into a 'potent creative tendency which has formed our universe', which touches the 'cutting edge of our ability to transcend ourselves, to create new and more spiritual directions in human evolution' (1980: 134).

The other two core conditions for therapeutic change set out by Rogers are our warmth and our genuineness. Warmth is the accepting, caring and 'prizing' of the other person. If the client experiences these attitudes coming from their social worker (or teacher, or simply another person), then they are more likely to feel confident, less afraid to reveal who they are and *develop* who they are. Genuineness on the part of the social worker is essential. It means that they are 'putting up no professional front or personal façade' (1980: 113) in the relationship. In other words, they are themselves.

For Rogers these three *ways of being*, empathic, warm and genuine, provided *the* nurturing climate. Together they created the relational conditions in which a person could feel safe and the optimal environment for personal change to take place. Like Maslow, Rogers believed that if an individual, *any* individual with almost *any* behavioural history, is placed in these relational circumstances then their actualising tendency becomes operative and the person will select positive and constructive ways of being even though they are free to choose any direction.

## EMPATHY WITH THE INNER WORLD – ATTENTION TO THE OUTER WORLD

It is the social worker's task to deal with clients' inner and outer worlds (Schofield 1998). Neither of these worlds is more important than the other. Together they provide social workers with a holistic assessment. They equip the worker to say 'what is going on' in the situation with which they are dealing. For example, it is of little use if a social worker empathises with a man's feelings about emotional cruelty in his childhood but fails to see that he is abusing his stepson in a similar way. But, conversely, understanding and risk-assessing this man's abusive behaviour in the present will be enhanced by knowing and understanding his feelings about his past experiences. This accessing of the inner world as a way of making sense of the outer world is the emotionally intelligent basis upon which to practise social work.

Engaging with the inner world of this client can guide our responses, helping us to pitch them at a level that is more likely to result in a constructive outcome. And, following Rogers, we may hope that our empathic responses towards him may facilitate his choosing more creative ways of managing his emotions and relating to his stepson.

Thus, social workers are two-dimensional workers: engaging with the outer, visible dimensions of life as well as inner, invisible ones. These two dimensions are represented in the words that social workers can use, and the ways in which they can verbally respond to their clients. Sometimes a response that refers to the outer world in practical, measurable terms is what is needed. At other times a response to the inner world, more nebulous and less measurable, will bring forth the better outcome. Neither response is better than the other: both have equal place in the social worker's toolkit.

There follow two case studies which make the distinction between outer and inner world responding. As you read the social worker's verbal responses think about how they are likely to affect what happens next. In what ways might they influence what the client says or does?

---

 **Case Study Three**

**Responding to inner or outer worlds of clients**

**Case A**

Imagine that you work in a Community Mental Health Team. A GP refers a patient, a 45-year-old man, and the doctor writes that, in his view, the patient 'should go out and meet people'.

*(Continued)*

---

*(Continued)*

You visit the patient. He is deeply depressed. He has been made redundant and some months ago his wife left, taking the children with her. He has seen little of them since and he is trying to fight for more contact through the court. He has been forced to move from the matrimonial home and he lives alone in a small maisonette provided by the council.

After he has described his situation you are left deciding how to respond verbally. Consider the following two ways:

(a) 'Your GP thinks that you ought to try to get out more. I wonder if you'd be interested in going to a day centre?'
(b) 'I suppose it might feel as though you've lost most of what you valued in your life?'

**Practical work based on Case A (Done with others)**

Discuss these verbal responses by the social worker and try to discern the different ways that they may affect what happens next in the encounter.

**Case B**

Imagine that you work in a Children and Families Team. You receive an anonymous referral about a single parent mother who (allegedly) 'is always shouting at her children'. You visit the house. There is a three-year-old there and, indeed, the mother screams at the child in front of you and holds her hand up, as if threatening to smack her. She says that she knows who has reported her, and asks you what you are going to do about it. Are you going to take her kid away? She asks you what you expect, when she's left alone to manage everything.

Among your choice of responses could be:

A   'I wonder if you would like more support with your child?'
B   'I wonder if it's tough sometimes, bringing up your daughter on your own?'

**Practical work based on case B (Done with others)**

Discuss these verbal responses by the social worker and try to discern the different ways that they may affect what happens next in the encounter.

**Learning from the case studies**

In general, Question A directs the client's attention to the 'outer world' of the day centre or 'support'. Unless these things are already in the minds of the clients the questions are likely to distract them from their 'inner world'.

Question B relates more to what is, metaphorically, already in the room in the sense of being in the clients' minds. The first client's inner world might dwell on what he has lost. The second client might be ever mindful of being alone yet holding great parental responsibilities.

Questions A and B will draw out different responses from the client.

Question A is 'closed', requiring only a 'yes' or 'no' type of reply.

Question B is more 'open', allowing the client more choice in what to reply. It opens up the chance of talking about their inner worlds, if that is what they choose to do.

Mostly, though not always, the answers to A type questions will naturally follow from B type questions. It is often more productive in the long term if 'answers' such as 'day centre' or 'support' emerge from the client rather than being suggested by the worker.

## EMPATHY, EMOTIONAL INTELLIGENCE AND SELF-AWARENESS

In Chapter 4 the focus was upon the importance of self-awareness in workers who enter into relationship based practice with their clients. Self-awareness is the key *intra*personal dimension of relational work.

In this chapter the attention has switched to the *inter*personal dimension of relationship based social work, focusing upon the theory of emotional intelligence and the practice of empathy.

These three dimensions – self-awareness, emotional intelligence and empathy – come together when a worker practises in a relational fashion. And when they are brought together in the mind and the behaviour of a worker, they form a formidable basis for practice in two key areas of social work: *therapy* and *assessment*.

### Therapy

Social workers frequently work with people whose referral concerns behaviours such as neglectful parenting or alcohol abuse, but often these clients' problems are caused by, or sustained by, disabling states of depression or anxiety (Ruch 2005). If social workers are to dig below the surface symptoms and access the underlying depressive and anxious states, then empathic communication is essential. The worker's mind must connect with that of the client (Howe 2008), for such a connection helps the client feel understood, and being understood by another person is the basis for understanding of oneself. The client's growth in self-understanding can be the springboard for his or her personal, therapeutic change.

Therapeutic social work therefore hinges upon empathic understanding. It requires emotional intelligence on the part of the social worker, the ability to perceive and facilitate emotions in others, and such skills are predicated upon the worker's prior ability to be emotionally intelligent with the *self*. We thereby see that self-awareness, emotional intelligence and empathy are interconnected – each requiring the other two for full effectiveness.

## Assessment

One of social work's primary duties is accurate assessment, perhaps of a person's needs, or the risk they pose, either to themselves or to others. And at the foundation of accurate assessment is communication. For example, there is evidence that some cases of fatal child abuse have been caused by poor communications between professionals and with clients (Reder and Duncan 2003). Seden (2005: 20) argues that good communication

> involves far more than imparting information. It is a process where thoughts, feelings, ideas and hopes are not only exchanged between people, but also need to be understood together.

Seden's point is that *understood* communication, which is essential to *accurate* assessment, is multi-faceted and will therefore include feelings as well as opinions. And as we have seen, the accessing of feelings is a very different activity from simply hearing someone's verbal expression of an opinion, for emotional access requires access to the self as well as the other person, and the three skills needed are those of self-awareness, emotional intelligence and empathy.

---

**Exercise Four**

**Empathy, self-awareness and emotional intelligence**

When we describe an event to a person we choose the extent to which we disclose our feelings. This choice will probably be affected by how well we know the person with whom we are speaking, or how much we trust them.

There follows an example of a life event described by a 21-year-old person who was 14 when it happened. There are two versions of the 'story': the first has no verbally expressed feelings, while the second has feelings added.

**Version 1 – Without verbally expressed feelings**

One evening when I was aged 14 my mother answered a ring at the door. It was the police. They said they had some news, and my mother asked them to come in. They told my mother that my brother, who was 18, had been in an accident on his motorcycle, and that he was in the A&E department of the hospital. My mother phoned my father, and we all met at the hospital. My brother had some injuries and he was unconscious. The doctors told us that the injuries would heal and that the main concern was the unconsciousness. In the following days we took it in turns, and he was visited at least twice a day. The nurses encouraged us to keep talking to my brother, but he didn't show any awareness of our presence. This went on for about 10 days, but then we noticed small differences. He began to react to our voices. It was weeks before he returned to normality and could hold a conversation with us. He had no memory at all of the accident but in other ways his memory was not affected. Now, seven years later, he is just as he always was.

---

### Version 2 – With verbally expressed feelings

One evening when I was aged 14 my mother answered a ring at the door. It was the police. **I remember feeling worried immediately. Before they said anything I just knew something was wrong.** They said they had some news, and my mother asked them to come in. They told my mother that my brother, who was 18, had been in an accident on his motorcycle, and that he was in the A & E department of the hospital. **I wanted to cry. He and I have always been close. But my mother stayed calm, and I followed her example.** My mother phoned my father, and we all met at the hospital. My brother had some injuries and he was unconscious. **It was horrible seeing him there, plugged into monitors. Again, the nurses and doctors around his bed were calm, and I held in my feelings.** The doctors told us that the injuries would heal and that the main concern was the unconsciousness. **I felt so anxious when I heard this. What did it mean? Would he ever get better? I couldn't sleep that night, and cried a lot.** In the following days we took it in turns, and he was visited at least twice a day. The nurses encouraged us to keep talking to my brother, but he didn't show any awareness of our presence. **It was so distressing. Someone I'd spent my life talking to couldn't reply to me. My parents were strong and hopeful, and I tried to be like them.** This went on for about 10 days, but then we noticed small differences. **That was a fantastic change!** He began to react to our voices. It was weeks before he returned to normality and could hold a conversation with us. **What a relief!** He had no memory at all of the accident but in other ways his memory was not affected. Now, seven years later, he is just as he always was. **I've thought lots about it since. I just feel as though our family was very fortunate.**

### Practical work 1: talking and empathic listening

In this exercise you can either describe an incident from your LIFELINE, or refer back to your genogram to describe the relationship that you have or had with one of the people on it. In either case, the life event or the relationship should have some emotional content.

### The role of the talker

Prepare what you want to say and, with a class partner, describe the life event or the person in a *factual* kind of way, omitting any reference to how you feel (as in Version 1 above).

### The role of the listener

Listen to your class partner with close attention (SOLER). Remember, you are not trying to work out what *you* would feel like if you experienced a life event like the one being described. Rather, you are trying to empathise with the person to whom you are listening.

### Practical work 2: empathic responding

1  Now, the listener should try to say what they 'heard' behind the spoken words and, using empathy, try to name the emotions that they guess the other person may have felt (and may still feel). In this situation empathy will take the form of

*(Continued)*

an intuitive and imaginative wondering about your partner's emotional experience. But beware! Empathic responding may be inaccurate. It is best to respond cautiously by saying, 'Perhaps I'm quite wrong about this, but I wonder if you felt... ?' This question may cause a person to correct your supposition, and thereby help them to become more aware of their actual feelings.

2 Next, talk with each other about how accurately the listener has *sensed* the feelings of the talker. Was it similar, or quite different?

Now swap roles, the listener becoming the talker and the talker becoming the empathic listener.

*Some points to consider:*

1 One of the main ways of achieving empathy is by partly letting go of oneself, one's suppositions and prejudices. These act as blocks to sensing the feelings of the other person, and in the next chapter more reference will be made to this.

2 The roots of empathy (Goleman 2006) lie partly in the 'attunement' between mother and child that was discussed in Chapter 3. In adult to adult relationships empathy still relies on one person adjusting himself to the other's *flow* – which means accurately picking up signals from the other without 'interference' from one's own mind. This is not always easy, and more will be said about it in the next chapter.

## CHAPTER SUMMARY

- The chapter built on Chapter 4 in that self-awareness is the key requirement for a deeper awareness of others, which has been the focus of this chapter.
- The emphasis has been on knowing your clients at both the cognitive and the emotional level. Each of these levels can 'tell' you things about your clients, helping you to build supportive and purposeful relationships and make assessments.
- The chapter used the concept of emotional intelligence as a way of facilitating, understanding and managing feelings.
- Through the use of a case study and an experiential exercise you were enabled to use and practise emotional intelligence.
- The chapter also explored the idea of empathy and provided you with a structured method of practising it.

 *Further reading*

Howe, D. (2008) *The Emotionally Intelligent Social Worker.* Basingstoke: Palgrave Macmillan. This book provides a rigorous application of the theory of emotional intelligence to relationship based social work practice.

Howe, D. and Hinings, D. (1995) 'Reason and emotion in social work practice', *Journal of Social Work Practice, 9(1)*: 5–14.
This article shows how social work practice and procedures are essentially based on rationality and can ignore the reality of the underlying emotionality and 'irrationality' of human motivation and interaction.

Koprowska, J. (2008) *Communication and Interpersonal Skills in Social Work.* Exeter: Learning Matters.
This book sets out the centrality of communication to effective social work practice. The writing combines communication theory with activities (often concerning self-awareness) for students to practise.

Rogers, C. (1980 [1963]) *A Way of Being.* Boston: Houghton Mifflin (in particular, Chapters 1, 6 and 7).
Roger writes this book from a highly personal stance, showing how he developed his theoretical framework of empathy, warmth and genuineness, and put it into practice.

Seden, J. (2005) *Counselling Skills in Social Work Practice.* Buckingham: Open University Press.
The author shows how counselling skills can be used effectively in contemporary social work.

# 6 SUSTAINING ONESELF IN RELATIONSHIP BASED SOCIAL WORK

## INTRODUCTION

Previous chapters have provided you with the opportunity to enhance your self-awareness by helping you to reflect upon the life experiences that have made you *who* you are. This chapter should help you to complement this subjective exploration by asking the more objective question about *what* you are (or will become) as a social worker. These two dimensions, *who* you are and *what* you are, form the bases of your training which requires your subjective self, your thoughts, feelings and behaviours, to engage gradually with the more objective role and identity called 'social worker'.

The Key Roles that you are practising are tools you use to do your job, but they are not one-off acquisitions. Rather they are a process, continuous and dynamic, because it is 'you' who is performing them, and you will change as you are challenged cognitively and emotionally by the human circumstances within which social workers carry out their tasks. This change is inevitable, but it is also part of your professional duty to develop yourself within your role. Your subjective personhood and your objective role are thus intertwined and never more so than when you set out to work in a relational manner which consciously and purposefully 'brings yourself' into your work.

The social work profession is organised in such a way that both your professional and your personal developments should be facilitated. For example, within the NOS (Key Role 6, 19.4) is the requirement to use supervision and support systems in order to reflect critically on your professional practice and performance. The standard also requires you to identify your own achievements, your strengths and your weaknesses. And at the personal level you are asked to become aware of what you need if you are to develop and enhance your ability to reflect on yourself and manage your stress. You are to review your stress levels and workload (Key Role 5, 14.1) and use supervision and support to discuss areas that might cause ethical conflict or hinder the relationship with your client (Key Role 1, 1.3). Thus the profession recognises the interacting dimensions of who you are and what you are, and agencies should provide support for and facilitate the development of these personal and professional aspects.

This chapter focuses upon three processes that can help the relational social worker to use and sustain the subjective self within the objective framework of the social work role. The first of these is reflective practice and the second is mindfulness. Both processes tend towards enhancing your personal development, although the distinction between this and professional development is not hard and fast. The third process is supervision and, in particular, that aspect of it which is concerned with sustaining the self as a relationship based practitioner. Again, this process will link together the professional and the personal.

As you engage with reflection, mindfulness and supervision, you will see that each complements the other two and, together, they should provide you with tools to facilitate the ongoing search for congruency between who you are as a person and what you are in your professional social work role. The processes facilitate a type of conversation between you as subject and your social work role as object, helping personhood fit professionhood so that tension between the two is minimised and professional practice is enhanced. They are also key processes in enabling social workers to prepare themselves for relationship based practice, promoting as they do an authentic professional persona which helps clients to experience and relate to the 'real person' behind the social work role.

As you work through the chapter it will help to bear in mind that reflection is concerned with looking back while mindfulness is concerned with attempting to keep your thoughts and feelings in the present. If you have the kind of mind that 'thinks' in diagrams, you can view this as a T shape – reflection focusing on and delving down to the 'there and then' of what has passed, and mindfulness concerned with the horizontal, the present 'here and now'.

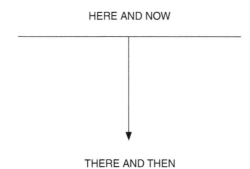

HERE AND NOW

THERE AND THEN

Reflection and mindfulness might be done alone or with others. Supervision involves the oversight of another person, and it can include reflection and mindfulness.

## REFLECTIVE PRACTICE: PONDERING PURPOSEFULLY ON WHAT HAS PASSED

To begin, the word 'reflection' will be used in a simple and literal sense. Reflection means to 'bend back'. Imagine that you are reading a novel. You arrive at a part where the plot is complicated, so you flick back through the pages to refer again to a passage that will help you to make sense of what you are reading now. In doing this you are reflecting, stopping your one-directional progress to return to what has already been seen. Sometimes we may 'look back' literally when, for example, climbing a steep hill we turn around and gaze down to where we started from. This physical action may cause our minds to 'reflect' in a more abstract way – perhaps by pondering the idea that we are making a mental journey as well as a physical one. Such pondering can lead to personal reflection, a bending back of our minds by returning mentally to an event or an experience, a thought or feeling from our past. In this way reflection can be a return to ourselves, a holding before us of an image that we have of what has passed, of who or what we were in the there and then.

Reflection is often an involuntary and sometimes an unwanted activity when, for example, we have an unpleasant memory on our mind that will not go away. But reflection can also be a disciplined and purposeful pursuit, a set-apart time when we bring deliberately into our minds events of the past day or week, and explore them in terms of how we feel or think about them, what we have learned from them, how we related to others within them, and so on. Reflection is used in several different ways in the social work literature (Knott and Scragg 2007) and many social work texts discuss the topic (e.g. Trevithick 2005). To introduce it here, and to link it with relationship based practice, a case study of Toby, a social worker, is provided. The study is based on the three-phase process of reflection set out by Boud and Knights (see Payne in Adams et al. 2002). The phases are :

A   returning to the experience;
B   attending to feelings connected with the experience;
C   re-evaluating the experience through recognising its outcomes and implications.

 **Case Study One – the process of reflection**

**The situation**

Toby is a social worker in a 'looked after children' team. It is the evening and his mind persists in returning to an event that happened during the day. He decides to 'give in' to his preoccupied mind, sit down, and deliberately and purposefully reflect on what happened.

**Phase 1: returning to what happened**

The dress code at work is casual but it is usual for workers to wear smarter clothes on certain occasions such as attending court. Toby had gone to work not expecting to need a jacket and tie but because someone else was ill he was asked to stand in at a court hearing to revoke a Care Order. His manager showed some irritation about his casual clothing and, in front of colleagues, told him that he should keep smarter clothes at the office in case of an unanticipated event such as this. At the time Toby felt angry with the manager and a bit put-down. He said nothing, but went home to change into more acceptable clothing.

**Phase 2: attending to feelings**

In reflecting on the event Toby quickly feels anger again, but why? In trying to make sense of his feelings he comes to see that he felt humiliated by the manager who could have chosen to speak with him alone, rather than in front of team members. On the other hand, he accepts that there is an 'unwritten rule' about wearing smarter clothes for court, and that colleagues do keep clothes at work for this purpose. To this extent the manager was 'right'.

As Toby reflects, so his anger begins to subside and his mind is able to turn more towards his manager's position. He knows that she has been working under pressure and has been unable to fill the team's vacancies for full time permanent staff. The gaps have been filled by agency workers, some of whom have left after a few months and before they have had time to build up experience of the children and families that they have worked with.

**Phase 3: re-evaluation, outcomes and implications**

Toby has become aware of his resistance to smarter clothing – a resistance that goes deeper than the events of this day. In 'smart' clothes he does not 'feel himself'. But he also reflects that sometimes a professional life makes demands that are in tension with one's preferred way of being, including the way one dresses. This, he notes, is a point to ponder on another occasion. But for now, he resolves to speak with his manager, acknowledge the tension there has been between them, and observe the team's practice of leaving clothing in the office.

**The process of reflection – learning points from the case**

Toby has 'bent back' to an event earlier in the day. He has *accessed his emotions* and *processed them cognitively*. He has also *put himself into the position of the other person* involved, *stood back* and *analysed*, and *become aware of the impact of his behaviour on others*. Through reflection he has engaged with the process of *seeking congruity between who* he is as a person *and what* he is as a social worker.

# LOCATING REFLECTIVE PRACTICE IN A WIDER SOCIAL WORK SETTING

The process of reflection described above started from a seemingly simple incident of tension between a manager and a team member. Through the discipline of reflection Toby was able to convert the unproductive fretting of his mind into a structured and creative process.

Within the process we can see implications in at least four dimensions:

1   Toby's relationship with his manager.
2   His relationship with himself as a person.
3   His relationship with himself as a social worker.

And these relationships will have effects on

4   His relationships with his clients because these are affected by the complementarity (or lack of it) between his personhood and his professionhood.

To these four dimensions we may also add a fifth insofar as Toby begins to reflect 'critically' (White et al. 2006) on the psychological effects that the wider, psychosocial question of worker recruitment is having on his manager and her team.

Reflection may bring with it rapid and constructive insights and outcomes, but not always. Sometimes it is possible for it to lead to discomfort and bring to clarity a personal or professional problem for which there is no immediate solution.

For example, reflective practice can expose the false certainties that may be created by working in a culture of NOS, government protocols and local authority procedures (Knott 2007: 7). These certainties define and channel social workers' experiences and actions. They can lead to a belief that workers have, or should have, 'solutions' to human problems whereas, for much of the time, they are limited to assessing and managing as creatively as they can the dilemmas that are brought to them. Likewise, the technical, theoretical analyses which social workers employ can tend to imply certainty (Thompson 2009) but, at best, they are imperfect tools to help social workers to struggle and 'puzzle their way forward' (Howe 2009: 206) amidst complex reality.

Ruch (2002) picks up on these points and sees the growing interest in reflective practice as a response to the 'technical-rational, competency-based approaches to professional education and practice'. She argues that reflective practice 'involves acknowledging precisely that which the competency culture avoids – the uniqueness of each situation encountered'. Her point is that social work cannot be reduced in a simplistic fashion to performance criteria because the emotions that are inherent in the human encounters of social work do not always fall in with the procedural rules set out by government and local authorities.

Thus, reflection can be a counterbalance to the protocols that increasingly drive social work practice and a foil to certainties that are based on simplistic and inadequate understanding. Reflection can bring social workers back to a realisation of the uniqueness of their relationships with their selves and with their clients, fostering a proper sense of humility and caution in the ways that they practise and exercise influence over other people's lives. Reflection can remind workers to be human, to retain and reveal compassion in circumstances that may also require them to act in formal and legalised ways.

Reflective practice is therefore an essential part of contemporary social work, reminding workers of what they should not forget, but easily can, amidst the demands of processes and protocols. It is a way of social workers constructively pondering their professional experiences and the emotions that are engendered by them. It can help workers to understand and sustain their self-in-role, to sense the tensions and incongruities between *who* and *what* they are. It is a method of workers naming these tensions and finding (or perhaps *not* finding) some way of accommodating themselves to their work in ways which remain faithful to the relational contacts and values which, perhaps, drew them towards a social work career.

## REFLECTION: SUSTAINING THE RELATIONAL SELF IN DISTRESSING CIRCUMSTANCES

Stress can affect workers, clients, carers and managers in the social work context, but stress is not entirely an individual affair because organisations such as social services exist within intrinsically stressful circumstances. Hoggett (2006) calls these circumstances 'contested' because welfare agencies are the focus of many different people's expectations and opinions about what they should be doing, and how they should do it. He argues that competing 'values and policies saturate all public organisations' and, because of this, social care services become 'engaged in the management of social anxieties and other collective sentiments which are partly conscious and partly unconscious'. It is, he argues, 'the fate of the public official...to contain the unresolved value conflicts and moral ambivalence of society'.

A primary example of this is child protection which, through government intervention in some high-profile cases, has become formally politicised. And this politicisation has drawn attention from the press, bringing safeguarding into a wider public debate and exercising influence over the ways in which 'abusers' are perceived and reified.

Thus, social workers may be involved with a particular child or family, but surrounding them is a politically charged atmosphere that is driven by (sometimes ill-informed) 'collective sentiments' about the abuse of children. How are social workers to sustain themselves in this atmosphere, to practise in accordance with occupational standards, protocol and statute, yet retain the interpersonal practice that lies at the heart of relational social work?

The following case study explores such tensions, showing how social workers can use reflection as a way of pondering purposefully on what has passed. Reflecting assists them in sustaining themselves. It helps them to stay in constructive relationships with themselves and with their clients, and with the environment of the social work profession.

---

 **Case Study Two**

**The background**

Imagine that you are a worker in a child protection team. At the beginning of last week you received into care Josie, a six-month-old baby who had cigarette burns around her genital area. You have had a hectic week that included a multi-agency

*(Continued)*

*(Continued)*

strategy meeting, making applications to the court, visits to the hospital and foster parents, interviews with Josie's mother and her partner, writing up case notes and discussions with your manager and colleagues.

**Now**

A week later, Josie is in foster care and the emergency aspects of the case are giving way to assessment and future planning. The evidence is that it was the mother's partner who inflicted the cigarette burns and although he has moved out of the house the decision for the short term at least is that the baby will remain in the foster home while the mother's ability to protect her child is assessed.

**Reflection: emotions and sense making**

During last week you had little time to think beyond the immediate tasks that confronted you, and you worked long hours. Your manager has asked you to take time off in lieu. You use part of the time to go back in your mind to the events of the last week. At first there is not much order to your reflection – your mind goes from thought to feeling without coherence. Previously contained emotions come to the surface. Mainly you feel distressed and angry.

What you most want to do is make sense of what happened. The question 'why?' is foremost in your mind. Why did someone do this to a baby? You feel irritated and impatient with yourself because you cannot explain it. It's true that you have received information from another local authority that Josie's mother's partner was brought up in care after experiencing abuse. But you know that this is inadequate as an expla-nation, though it might contribute towards one. You add to your self-irritation when the word 'evil' keeps coming into your mind. Isn't this a word that some journalists might use to describe this behaviour, and isn't it an unhelpful word for a trained and experienced social worker to use? You chastise yourself for thinking in this way and you ponder the process of using words to project on to others what we fear within ourselves. You wonder if you could be doing this. Given certain circumstances, could you physically harm another person? You let this thought flow in your mind, without seeking to deny its possibility, and your thinking reminds you of Milgram's experi-ments (Milgram 1974; also Zimbardo 2008) and the idea that *all* people are capable of thinking or behaving in ways that damage others but that some people, for reasons that are not always known, move beyond thought to action.

At this stage in the reflective process you decide to let thoughts and feelings intermingle and follow on, one from the other, without attempting to shape or control them. You find it soothing and cathartic.

**Re-evaluating the experience**

You have let your mind bend back and wander with a purpose, and you have located your specific experiences of this case within a larger framework of meanings and constructions about human conduct. Now you can see that however much you, as a social worker, want firm explanations for events, you are destined to work always with uncertainty. Explanations are partial and provisional – not least because information is incomplete or may be inaccurate. You accept that you may never have satisfactory answers to your 'why' questions. But the reflective process, though seemingly muddled and disorderly, has helped to clear your mind of the first involuntary feelings of distress and anger, and it leaves you freer to focus on your role with Josie. You remind yourself of your primary task of protecting her and making what arrangements you can to maximise her developmental prospects. This clarity of thinking and ease of feeling provides you with a refreshed emotional and cognitive state of mind for your return to work. You feel that you have arrived at a proportionate perspective on the past week and this is a positive foundation for the sensitive, relational work that must be carried out with Josie's mother and, maybe, her partner.

**Outcomes and implications: preparing the self for relationship based practice**

In your reflection you deliberately bring to mind your relationship values, of engaging with clients in an unprejudiced manner and assessing their behaviours rather than judging them as people. The reflective process has freed you in your mind to relate to them in ways that are open to possibilities, not attaching to them negative labels or carrying with you pre-judged outcomes that would act as a block to listening and empathy.

Overall, the reflective process has helped you to obtain a calm and measured perspective on the events of the last week, and this helps you to sustain yourself and prepare you for relationship based practice.

# REFLECTION: GENERAL LEARNING POINTS ILLUSTRATED BY THE SPECIFIC EXAMPLE

The example above of a social worker reflecting on a child protection case illustrates a general point that reflection often concerns three types of relationships. These are:

**1   Your relationship with yourself**

Here you may explore your thoughts and feelings. It is not unusual to experience a feeling of disorder with thoughts and feelings tumbling into awareness, but allowing this process to continue is likely to result in greater clarity. Sometimes you will be led into analysing the effects on you of what has happened, and this may include your relationship with others or with your environment. Primarily, this part of the reflection process is about self-awareness and, after a period of demanding or stressful work, it is about sustaining the self, regaining energy and a sense of your personal and professional identities in relation to others and your work.

**2   Your relationship with others**

By 'others' is meant your clients, your managers and team colleagues, and workers in other agencies with whom you co-operate. Reflection may reveal tensions, professional disagreements or points of harmony with these others. It is a way of clarifying your own thoughts, of trying to understand why other people think differently, and attempting to empathise with their position without losing your own.

### 3 Your relationship with your environment

By 'environment' is meant the totality of inanimate things that influence or control your work. These can be your agency, your professional body (GSCC) and other organisations, laws and protocols, theories, prevailing explanations of behaviour, values and attitudes, and so on. It may simply be the office layout or, as in the example of Toby, the clothing that you are expected to wear. Again, you may experience this environment as facilitative of you as a person and a professional or, sometimes, it might seem restrictive or even antithetical to your work. Reflection can reveal and clarify such tensions.

Reflection cannot always provide 'answers' to problems, but it usually leads towards greater clarity – perhaps revealing the right questions to ask of yourself or others. It has been seen that reflection means 'bending back': it is an activity in the present which is oriented to the past. But sometimes it can lead to future planning (though not strictly part of reflection it is hard to stop the brain moving to what has not yet happened). Reflection is also a preparatory foundation for checking your perceptions with another person such as a superviser – a process to be explored later in the chapter.

While reflection is essentially about pondering upon the there and then – on what has passed – the process of mindfulness is concerned with attempting to experience oneself and one's environment in the here and now. It has an important place in relationship based practice and, together with reflection, is a building block for supportive supervision.

## MINDFULNESS: PONDERING WITH PURPOSE ON THE PRESENT MOMENT

### What is mindfulness?

Social work is among the most privileged occupations, offering as it does an intimate connection with our fellow human beings in their times of stress, incapacity and illness. These connections with others are enriched when social workers are connected with themselves. The process of mindfulness has this self-connection at its heart, but insists that we cannot truly connect with ourselves through the past or the future, but only in the here and now (Kabat-Zinn 1994).

The minds of social workers tend to be occupied either with the past, such as when they are assessing what has been, or with the future when they are helping to make plans for people's lives. The present moment can be lost between what was and what will be. This is particularly true of those occasions when social workers have their body in one place and their mind in another – looking at their watch and hoping that they will not be late for their next appointment. This way of conducting one's working life has been described as a state of paying 'continual partial attention' (Linda Stone, quoted in Kabat-Zinn 2005: 157) to several things at once – a condition that is contrary to holding focused attention on one person or thing.

In circumstances such as these, which are not unusual in social work practice, it is difficult for workers to experience themselves as a unity of body and mind. Instead, feelings of fragmentation can become the norm as the demands to think about many things at once or be in more than one place at the same time build up. But such normal social work situations take on more complexity for relationship based workers who are attempting to engage empathically with the emotions that are present in their transactions with their clients. Intense exposure of the self to the emotions of others, and mentally moving from one person's emotions to another's, can afterwards leave workers feeling that their clients are, metaphorically, living in their mind. At times like this workers require a method of mentally disentangling themselves from others, of discovering what is real and true about themselves as a discrete and unique person. Mindfulness can offer this.

Mindfulness is an experience that is the opposite of multi-tasking and, unlike reflection which deliberately draws on what *has* happened, mindfulness is focused on what *is* happening in present time. Kabat-Zinn (1990: 60) sums this up by describing it as a 'human endeavour…that does not involve trying to get somewhere else but, rather, emphasises being where you already are'. Because mindfulness is an attempt to *be* in a certain way there is an understandable reluctance to analyse it, for analysis would require stepping outside to *examine* the being, thereby losing the mental state of staying *inside* the experience. However, among those who have written about it there is some consensus that mindfulness may be broken down into three parts: *awareness* of *present experience* with *acceptance* (Germer 2005: 7). The following case study illustrates these three parts of mindfulness.

 **Case Study Three**

**Ruminating on a case**

Hope is a 26-year-old black Zimbabwean social worker who specialises in adoption. Because of his partner's change of job he has recently moved from an inner city team to work in a predominantly white rural area of Britain. He was relieved to move because he had been suffering from stress and depression, and he saw the new job and area as making a fresh start.

He is undertaking a Form F assessment (an assessment procedure undergone by prospective adoption or foster parents) with a white, British couple. On his first visit to the adoption applicants he felt a coolness, but he didn't think much about it. But now, having completed his third visit, he feels antipathy from them. Nothing that is directly hostile is said or done. It is more that Hope feels it in the atmosphere. His attempts to build rapport feel as though they're being rebuffed.

It begins to play on his mind. What is it about? Is it racial prejudice? He has no evidence for that. Is it that they resent the power that they may perceive him having over them? Hope doesn't know the answers to these questions. But the process of

*(Continued)*

*(Continued)*

thinking about them seems to be causing his mind to race in unproductive ways. He begins to feel stressed and recognises the negative and irrational trains of thought running through his mind as possible precursors of the depression to which he is vulnerable.

He decides to stop analysing the situation and asking himself questions which he cannot answer. Instead he becomes mindful of himself.

### Self-awareness and moving towards present experience

Hope knows that he is vulnerable to stress when his body and his mind seem to lose synchronicity. It is most apparent with his breathing when it becomes erratic, or his thoughts cause him to believe that he cannot fill his lungs.

He knows that if he regulates his breathing by letting his mind become aware of it, concentrating first on the in-breath and then on the out-breath, his concentrating mind and his breathing body will achieve balance in an activity that is essential to life. Hope does his breathing exercises. Through them his mind (attention) and body (lungs) re-establish their relationship: metaphorically he is putting them in the 'same place at the same time'. Each time Hope's mind drifts back to the fostering situation he lets it remain there momentarily, then brings it back to focus on his breathing.

In doing this he becomes aware of his experience in the present 'real time'. His experience is of his real and true self – a unique and discrete person.

### Acceptance

Acceptance is self-compassion (Gilbert 2009). Hope tries to focus on a non-judgemental kindliness towards himself, accepting his experience as it is, not how he expected it to be, thought it should be, or how other people might want it to be. Obtaining some mastery over his body's breathing transfers to experiencing an enhanced degree of mastery over his mind. He knows from past experience that if he treats himself as an interacting whole of body and mind, he is likely to feel more whole. Now the questions about the adoption applicants are less pressing. No answers have been found, but none are yet needed.

He has stilled himself. His mind is no longer racing. His automatic thoughts have ceased. He feels ready, if he chooses, to reflect on this case in a calm and rational fashion – staying open to uncertainty rather than demanding answers from himself.

Learning points to take from the case study are that, with practice, social workers can undertake a process of mindfulness which re-forms their self into a person who feels more unified, rather than one who is fragmented by self-doubt and criticism, and whose persistent thoughts are guesses about what other people think. In this way mindfulness can be used to re-establish a constructive relationship between parts of the self, body, mind and spirit (Matthews 2009), and, as with Hope, it can be a preparation for undertaking personal and professional reflection.

The connection between self and others is thematic to relational work so that, just as the heart of social work is 'looking after' people, so workers must also 'look after' themselves, and this is one function of mindfulness. Mindfulness is a way of workers giving to themselves those same qualities that they would extend to their clients, a respect and tolerance, a reluctance to rush to judgement without an understanding that is qualified by self-compassion and a deep awareness of the vulnerabilities and frailties that are endemic in being human.

## WRITING – REFLECTIVELY AND MINDFULLY

Methods such as routine journal keeping or occasional writing can assist in reflection and mindfulness. Writing can combine past and present tense, processing the emotional, cognitive and somatic self through time and, while doing it, the writer is 'grasping ideas and images out of thin air' (Bolton, undated website entry) and thereby experiencing the self in realities that are quite different from the daily routines of which we are conscious.

Writers may seek to put on to paper words about what is *really* happening in their lives and the very process of writing can bring clarity, producing a document that can be read, re-read and revised in an iterative process.

Here is an example from Dr Becky Ship's writing called 'A Letter to My Patients,' (in Bolton 2001: 158).

> *A Letter to My Patients*
> I am listening, really I am.
> I have to be honest, though – sometimes it's hard to pay attention. If my focus seems to shift away from you to the clock, or the door, or the computer, please don't think it's because I don't care.
> Let me tell you something, my friend. I've got problems, too. Sometimes my problems are bigger than yours and I'm hanging on by my fingernails. But I'm the one with the desk and the prescription pad.
> And what am I doing while you struggle to explain yourself to me? I'm holding myself together, is what I'm doing. I might distractedly put my hand up to my face while your words hover between us. Just checking I'm in one piece.
> I'm not painting my toenails, that's for sure.
> I'm not snuggled up under my duvet, drifting off to sleep.
> I'm not licking a rapidly melting chocolate ice cream cone.
> I'm sitting here, listening to you.
> So make the most of me.

Becky Ship provides an honest account of wanting to be mindfully present with a person, actively listening to their problems, but instead she experiences her mind wandering involuntarily into her personal feelings. Her description is one of the commonplace experience of disintegration between the professional and the personal.

The writer reflects on her self and on her patient. Sometimes she is in present time ('I'm holding myself together', 'I'm sitting here') but the account seems to be a reminder that the present 'now' quickly slips into past – so her advice to her patient is to 'make the most' of it.

Such reflective and mindful writing can locate the self-as-person and self-in-role. It can help to integrate the two even if, in fact, it reveals the tensions between them by, for example, noting 'it's hard to pay attention'. Such honesty with the self (and perhaps with chosen others) can help to sustain the self-in-role by reminding a worker that she, like her clients, is human, fragile, and may on some days find it hard to cope.

Another example of reflective and mindful writing (Bolton 2001: 164) comes from Colin Feltham, the head of an academic counselling department. The following is an extract from his writing and, in a section not given in the quote that follows, he accuses himself of not being a good example to his students or clients because, though in the business of teaching other people to suffer less, he clearly suffers himself. He describes himself as 'divorced, demoralised, struggling to survive everyday anxiety, nobody's model' and disheartened by the bureaucratisation of his work. And he reflects that although he knows all the theory, and he has had the therapy, he is suffering more. Then, in an example of present tense mindfulness, he writes:

> Pained instinct turns me towards poignant music and stillness. I listen and sit, alone. Even in the midst of panic...I yield to the simplicity of my body's sitting breathing. Sometimes facial muscles twitch oddly; sometimes tears spring forth, roll down; often worries echo through my head. I am not exactly my own best friend, it's rather that now I am briefly reminded that life itself is friendly. Beyond the crucifixion of everyday adversity, there all along, is original peace.

It is as if Feltham has been helped by music to get in touch with his moment which brings some respite, self-sustenance and the awareness that such moments are possible for him. Pure mindfulness, the awareness of present experience with acceptance may be impossible to achieve and, in Colin Feltham's account, we see what are perhaps somatic signs of non-acceptance (tears, muscle twitches), emotions that worry him, and the cognitive realisation that he is not his own best friend.

The writings of Ship and Feltham are authentic inasmuch as they describe what it is to be human, the ways of presenting our selves to others, and times of self-honesty in which the gap between public personas and private realities is laid bare. This process of authenticity (that is, of authoring about oneself), however it is done, is a necessary part of achieving self-awareness and self-honesty. And it is this knowledge of the truth about who we are that allows us to relate in honest but measured ways in our professional practice. This is what our clients need from us; as Social Work at its Best (GSCC 2008) reminds us, 'people particularly value the human qualities contained in social work relationships'.

Reflection attempts to achieve clarity about what has passed, and mindfulness attempts to clarify and accept with compassion 'who we are' in the present time.

Taken together, these two processes provide sound bases of knowledge and experience for the practice of supervision.

## SUPERVISION: INTRODUCTION

One sentence from the QAA Benchmark for Social Work (2008, 4.6) sums up much of the purpose of supervision as it applies to relationship based practice. It requires social workers to 'recognise and work with the powerful links between intrapersonal and interpersonal factors and the wider social, legal, economic, political and cultural context of people's lives'.

The sentence make clear that social work always takes place within three interacting contexts: the small scale interpersonal and intrapersonal, and the large scale directives of social policy, legal and protocol frameworks, professional standards and values, and budget allocations. Relationship based practice is primarily small scale, emphasising as it does the qualitative aspects of the worker–client relationship but, of course, it is not immune from the influences of the larger scale socio-economic and political decisions that affect the whole of the social work profession. Relational practice may also be affected by temporary waves of public opinion about what social workers should be doing in contentious areas such as child protection, an example being the rise in the number of Care Orders granted after the publicised death of a neglected and abused child (*Daily Telegraph*, 6 December, 2008).

In discussing supervision as a tool for sustaining the worker's own self in relationship based practice the focus will be on the small scale perspective in social work, the interpersonal and intrapersonal dimensions, but it should be borne in mind how these can be affected by the kinds of large scale demands that influence managers' decisions when discharging their responsibility to ensure workers' accountability to the agency, quality-control their work, and manage resources in such a way that the work can be done.

Within the small scale perspective it should also be borne in mind that there are many variables that may influence supervision. Among them are the agency's function, the relationships and morale within the team, the superviser's style and interests, the management of local budgets, and the superviser–supervisee relationship. This last variable can be affected in some multi-disciplinary agencies by social workers being supervised by non-social-work staff although, as Wilson et al. (2008) point out, arrangements are often made that enable social workers to have social work supervision. This, they observe, may shift the balance away from the dominance of supervision by non-social-work managers. Another related development noted by Peach and Horner is that in the mental health services 'those who provide *clinical* supervision may not necessarily be the line manager of the supervisee' (2007: 229, their emphasis). In this way what Kadushin (1985) called the 'managerial' functions of supervision may be separated from the 'educational' and 'supportive' functions. There are many other variables which could become relevant to supervision discussions or outcomes such as the superviser's or supervisee's colour, gender, age, sexual orientation, religion or social class.

It is clear from this brief survey of supervision that it can never be a uniform experience for social workers. There are always elements involved that are unique to the agency or its workers, and supervisee and superviser will each bring to the meeting their individual selves. But, within this necessary uniqueness and with regard to relational practice, the one essential ingredient of supervision is the interacting between *what* you are as a social worker-in-role, and *who* you are as a person.

Thus, it is the task of relationship based supervision to explore and nurture co-operation between your subjective self and your objective role. Like all social workers, those who practise relationally carry out procedures, often as a function-ary of laws and protocols. On occasions they may be required to make arrange-ments that deprive clients of their liberty. But what distinguishes relational practice is the attempt to ensure that the worker's unique personhood is not lost in the pro-cedure or, in the extreme, the person of the social worker is not experienced by the client as being the same as the procedure itself. And so, supervision for relationship based practice is attempting to affirm the personhood of the social worker within their role, and discover how they can use this personhood most effectively in the service of their clients. It is these things that will form the primary focus of what follows. The discussion will be based upon an adapted version of the three functions of supervision in the analysis of Hawkins and Shohet (2006). The functions are *developmental, resourcing* and *qualitative*.

## THE DEVELOPMENTAL FUNCTION IN RELATIONSHIP BASED SUPERVISION

At the heart of the developmental function of supervision is enhancing the 'skills, understanding and capacities of the supervisees ...through reflection on, and explo-ration of, the supervisee's work with their clients' (Hawkins and Shohet 2006: 57). The role of the superviser may include helping the supervisee to:

- understand the client better;
- become more aware of their own reactions and responses to the client;
- understand the dynamics of how they and their client were interacting;
- look at how they intervened and the consequences of their interventions;
- explore other ways of working with this and other similar client situations.

The purposes here are to provide a regular time for supervisees to reflect upon the *content* and the *process* of their work, and receive feedback on it, to develop under-standing and skill, and receive information and another perspective on the situation (Hawkins and Shohet 2006: 58–59). It is similar to Kadushin's category of 'educational' supervision which is concerned with teaching the knowledge, skills, and attitudes necessary for the performance of clinical social work tasks through the detailed analysis of the worker's interaction with the client. (1985: 139)

From the work of Kadushin and Hawkins and Shohet we see that the developmental function is based upon the supervisee's needs to *understand* intellectually what is happening in the case. Discussion will take place about theories (Payne 2005, Oko 2008, Howe 2009) that help to explain a client's behaviours, or states of mind. And based upon theoretical explanations, thought will be given to effective interventions.

Essentially, this dimension of supervision is cognitive, appealing to reasoned analysis of the data. For Kadushin (1985) it may involve training, sharing of knowledge and experiences, advising, suggesting or helping workers solve problems. It is in contrast to the resourcing function which puts the focus on the emotional content of work.

## THE RESOURCING FUNCTION IN RELATIONSHIP BASED SUPERVISION

Hawkins and Shohet (2006: 58) see resourcing as 'a way of responding to how any workers engaged in personal work with clients are necessarily allowing themselves to be affected by the distress, pain and fragmentation of the client, and how they need time to become aware of how this has affected them and to deal with any reactions'.

Resourcing is therefore concerned with providing workers with the emotional resources they need in order to be a human resource for their clients. It helps social workers in the management of their emotions and tries to create the circumstances in which emotional intelligence can flourish. If it can achieve this aim there will be direct and beneficial consequences for clients because the ways in which workers practise are changed. Howe (2008: 187) makes the argument in this way:

Organisational cultures that value reflective, emotionally attuned practice also sponsor interventions that are constructive...It is not only odd but extraordinarily remiss that so few social workers have reflective supervision, particularly given the emotionally demanding and stressful nature of their work. If organisations fail to support, 'hold' and 'contain' their workers, they are in danger of blunting, even destroying the most important resource they have – the emotionally intelligent, available and responsive social worker.

Howe's argument is predicated on the belief that workers *are* the resource and (along with other, material resources) they require maintaining by the agency if they are to sustain themselves in the emotionally rough arena of contemporary social work practice. A primary task here is the role of supervision in containing workers' anxieties (Agass 2005) that are generated by the nature of their tasks. The argument is paralleled in Kadushin's chapter on 'supportive supervision' where workers' 'dissatisfaction with interpersonal supervision resulted from failures in the human-relations responsibilities of the superviser' in a context where 'the medium of service offered is the worker herself' (Kadushin 1985: 226–227).

This model of supervision requires supervisers to engage when appropriate with the emotions of their supervisees, seeing this engagement as a cathartic act that will facilitate the expression of feeling and, thereby, bring renewed strength and, perhaps, cognitive understanding in complex cases where emotion can cloud clarity. It is a model that validates the 'who' of the person and the 'what' of the worker, seeing them in some ways as interdependent. It attempts to 'plan and utilise their *personal and professional* resources better' (Hawkins and Shohet 2006: 59, their emphasis) thereby, again, engaging with the idea and reality that personhood and professionhood are intertwined in relational practice.

It seems that if agencies want to foster reflective and mindful practitioners then they must mirror reflection and mindfulness in the supervisory process. 'Reflective supervision produces reflective practice,' states Elizabeth Ash (1995: 26) and in writing this she is restating an idea that goes back some decades in social work. For example, Robinson (1978: 266) argued that (in relation to social work students):

> Since supervision...teaches a helping process, it must itself be a helping process so that the student experiences in his relation to his superviser a process similar to the one he must learn to use with his client.

Here, the processes between worker and superviser in the privacy of the agency should bear at least some resemblance to what happens in the outside world between worker and client. In such ways a *culture* of resourced practice is nurtured in which team members, managers and workers relate to one another by using the same values and facilitative ways of being that they would adopt with the people who use their services.

Adams et al. (2009: 381) reinforce the argument thus:

> Supervision...should provide support and an opportunity to express feelings and go 'below the surface' in the analysis of problems and situations. It should address particular issues that workers identify as problematic, including facing pain, anxiety, confusion, violence and stress.

And to this we may add that a resourcing agency will be one that can respond creatively to the difficult emotions that such a style of supervision can provoke. If it is an agency that facilitates feelings it must also be one that has the capacity and the skills to cope with circumstances where workers may 'become over full of emotions... produced through empathy with the client or re-stimulated by the client, or be a reaction to the client. Not attending to these emotions', warn Hawkins and Shohet (2006: 58) 'soon leads to less than effective workers, who become either over-identified with their clients or defended against being further affected by them' (see also Mattinson 1975, Rustin 2005). A team culture in which personal distress can be expressed and explored leads us to the qualitative function of supervision.

# THE QUALITATIVE FUNCTION IN RELATIONSHIP BASED SUPERVISION

Peach and Horner (2007: 229) express concern about the danger of 'the essentially supportive elements of classical supervision' being 'compromised at the expense of managerial surveillance'. It is clear that the word 'surveillance' is used pejoratively to describe situations in which 'managerialist imperatives' (Postle 2007) are in tension with sensitive and ethically sound social work. By contrast, Hawkins and Shohet argue that the manager's supervisory task of ensuring that the supervisee's quality of work 'is appropriate and falls within defined ethical standards' should be experienced as a positive and affirming part of the supervision process. They point out that a worker's failings in these areas may not be due to a lack of competence or training but can result from 'our inevitable human failings, blind spots, areas of vulnerability from our own wounds and our own prejudices' (2006: 58).

Here, again, is a reminder that all of us lack self-awareness in some areas of our life and sometimes this lack can have a negative effect on our ability to assess accurately and work effectively with a human situation. Such an effect is picked up by the 'quality control' of a sensitive and skilled superviser who will usually attempt to help the supervisee to become aware of and remedy the blocks to perception.

For example, in complex social work cases it is not difficult for a worker to arrive in a position where they have unknowingly taken into themselves feelings that 'belong' to their clients, and such psychological transactions can be the root of emotional confusion in the supervisee. But, with careful listening, a superviser may detect when such confusion is present – especially if the supervisee is displaying signs of it in the supervision session. In such a situation the superviser needs a mindfulness of the present or, as Trevithick suggests, a

> looking at the supervision session and what is happening in the here and now, particularly with a view to seeing if issues in relation to the service user are being replayed in the supervision session. (Trevithick 2005: 254)

Thus, the qualitative function of supervision requires an exploration of the worker's relationship with his or her clients, the asking of critical questions about its purposes, the needs that are being met within it, and how appropriate this is with regard to agency function and responsibilities. Such qualitative supervision is necessary for relationship based social work. It can serve to disentangle client from worker, to guard against emotional enmeshment in the relationship that clouds the purposes and the methods of the work.

Relational supervision, using the three foci of developing, resourcing and quality, attempts to enhance and sustain the constructive relationship between worker and client. The supervisory process should itself be a relationship based activity, mirroring between superviser and supervisee the qualities of relationship based social work. It does this by the superviser attending to the *who* of the supervisee that is performing the *what* of the social work role, exploring tensions between personhood and professionhood, and always with a focus on meeting clients' assessed needs in ways that are consistent with agency function and wider considerations of protocols and legislation. Thus, supervision is an essential and disciplined method of a worker sustaining the self in relational practice, and offering the self as a resource for others.

The principle operating here is stated by the Children's Workforce Development Council when they write that

> People who use social care and children's services say that services are only as good as the person delivering them. They value workers who have a combination of the right human qualities as well as the necessary knowledge and skills. *Supervision must enable and support workers to build effective professional relationships...* (CWDC 2007, emphasis added)

## CHAPTER SUMMARY

- The chapter focuses on relationship based practice bringing together who you are as a person with what you are as a social worker.
- The processes of reflection, mindfulness and supervision take a social worker through the three dimensions of time.
- Reflection concentrates on what happened with self and others in the past, mindfulness is focused upon what is happening in the present, and supervision, while including past and present, also looks to the future in terms of planning what should happen next.
- Each of these processes, in its different way, sustains the person of the worker. They integrate personhood and professionhood so that who you uniquely are, the part of you that relates to others and to whom others relate, is brought into co-operation with what you are as a social worker – with all that this means in terms of professional codes, protocols and legislative procedures.
- When this happens, clients experience you both as competent in your work and as a compassionate and understanding human being.

 *Further reading*

Bolton, G. (2001) *Reflective Practice: writing and professional development.* London: Paul Chapman Publishing.
The author shows how writing can lead to an enhanced and clarified understanding of the self, of others, and of situations.

Gilbert, P. (2009) *The Compassionate Mind.* London: Constable.
This author discusses the importance of compassion with the self (and others) – especially for those who work in a therapeutic context. More can be discovered through the website: http://www.compassionatemind.co.uk/

Knott, C. and Scragg, T. (eds) (2007) *Reflective Practice in Social Work.* Exeter: Learning Matters.
This book sets out theoretical understandings of reflective practice and helps you to apply them to your own experience and to aspects of social work practice.

# THE ETHICS OF RELATIONSHIP BASED SOCIAL WORK

## INTRODUCTION

When students are asked about their motivations to become social workers they frequently say that they want a job in which they are 'helping people'. Sometimes they have had experience of a helping role and it is this that has started them thinking about making social work their career. But, as well as this practical experience and thought, their motivations are often based on impulsive elements – expressions of unchosen inner drives to work in a helping capacity.

Social work education has the task of honing and directing these drives so that they become informed and transformed by the disciplines of theory, practical experience and professional ethics. But with regard to relationship based practice it is of crucial importance that the educational process also keeps alive the impulsive and untrained prompting to 'help others' that first gave emotional impetus to students' career decisions. This chapter will discuss why emotional impulses play a central part in the ethics of relationship based practice and it will also help you to locate or relocate these feelings within yourself.

The learning objectives of the chapter are to explore why principle based ethics, virtue ethics and the ethics of care are all, in their different ways, consistent with relationship based social work and the use of self. However, the chapter gives prominence to virtue ethics and the ethics of care because these ideas take into account both the rational and the emotional dimensions of human existence. By using case studies and concepts such as being in service, and letting oneself become a transitional object for a client, you should become more aware of how relationship based social workers may carry ethics within them. In this way using the self and acting ethically become integrated.

## SOCIAL WORK, PRINCIPLE AND UTILITARIAN BASED ETHICS

Social work is an ethically based activity because social workers are routinely involved in making decisions that affect people's physical, psychological and social well-being. These are always ethical matters. But social work ethics may be approached in different ways – all having in common a focus on deciding what is the 'right' thing to do in a situation.

One approach which is often used in social work education and practice is that of acting in accordance with principles. For example, it is a principle that workers should not discriminate between people on the basis of factors such as race, religion or sexuality. Equally, social workers should be aware of the power they have, and avoid using it in a way that is oppressive of others. Thus, 'anti-discriminatory' and 'anti-oppressive' may be understood as guiding principles for social work practice, just as the 'paramountcy' principle exists to ensure that in childcare proceedings the child's welfare comes before all else. In these contexts the word *principle* means a rule of practice that should be observed in all circumstances.

The moral philosophy of Immanuel Kant (1724–*c*.1803) has been highly influential in applying principles to professional ethics. His intention was to set out general 'categorical imperatives' concerning moral behaviour that were acquired through reason and would, therefore, become a binding duty on all reasonable persons. Perhaps the best known statement of such an imperative is to 'act only on that maxim [or principle] by which you can at the same time will that it should become a universal law' (Hill 2006). If we apply the principle to a social work example we can see that an abuser (who is rational and not masochistic) cannot obey this imperative *and* continue to abuse for, if he did, then all others would be entitled to abuse him and each other with impunity.

Principles are general frameworks to guide action and, by their nature, cannot provide detailed and unerring guidance about what to do in specific situations. For example, the British Association of Social Workers (BASW), in discussing ethics, advocates the principles of respect for 'human rights' and clients' 'self-determination'. The BASW code states that social workers should assist clients in developing their 'potential'. While these objectives are laudable, and lie at the heart of ethical social work practice, in themselves they cannot tell you *exactly* how a client's self-determination should be assisted, and how to know what is 'right' when one person's self-determination may come at the cost of restricting another person's life chances. Equally, the NOS for Social Work (NOS for Social Work 2004: 4) state that social workers must 'put individuals, families, carers, groups and communities first' but, in practice, an individual social worker might find that these categories of people are exercising competing claims on his department's finite resources in such a way that only one of them can come first. Thus, although principles are essential to social work ethics, like any one ethical system they cannot resolve completely the practice dilemmas that are part of a social worker's everyday life.

Principles set out to guide you in what you *ought to do* while another system of ethics places emphasis on the anticipated *consequences* of what you intend doing. The operating principle here is that actions should be taken on the basis of obtaining the greatest 'good' or 'happiness' for the greatest number of people. This way of thinking about practical ethics, called *utilitarianism*, is also concerned with individual and social justice in the sense that the 'greatest good' might be understood as ensuring that society's wealth is distributed fairly among people (Banks 2006). Like all ethical systems, utilitarianism has its flaws. For example, the simple notion of shaping social policy on the basis of the greatest good for the greatest number has difficulty in taking into account minorities whose lives might be impaired at the expense of benefiting the majority. Since its foundation in the 19th century, utilitarian philosophers have striven to overcome these kinds of difficulties, and the philosophy has greatly influenced social care and health policies in Britain. (Students who wish to know more about how principle based and utilitarian ethical systems can be applied to social work practice should consult more specialist literature, e.g. Hugman 2005, Banks 2006).

## VIRTUES, THE ETHICS OF CARE AND THE DEVELOPMENT OF CHARACTER

Both principle based and utilitarian based philosophies are important guides to social work practice and policy, but both can be criticised because they are what Held (2006) describes as 'moral enquiries that rely entirely on reason and rationalistic deduction'. By this she means that the assumption behind the word 'principle' is that the task of ethical theory is, through the use of reason, to arrive at generalised codes of behaviour that will be agreed upon by rational men and women. Likewise, a utilitarian decision is, in theory at least, based upon a rational analysis of what is the desirable outcome of a given human situation. For Held and others (e.g. Gilligan 1993, Noddings 2002) neither of these ways of thinking through ethics takes into account the uniqueness of small-scale human relationships, and this is why they argue that an 'ethics of care' is required which, in Held's words (2006: 539, my emphasis), 'appreciates the *emotions* and *relational capabilities* that enable morally concerned persons in *actual interpersonal contexts* to understand what would be best'. An example of the distinction being made by Held is that of assisted suicide where a 'rational' attitude taken by an emotionally detached law-maker could be quite different from that taken by the carer who each day witnesses the despair and lack of a will to live in a chronically or terminally ill person.

In ways such as this emotions and emotional intelligence come into ethics, usually in the context of interpersonal human relations, and this has been associated with the influence of feelings that are 'not up to us' (Slote 2006: 225). In other words, the ethics of care engages with the involuntary and non-rational nature of emotions, and with the idea that a person may care about others because their compelling inner feeling, and not an external principle, urges it upon them. It is a way of practising ethics that gives credence and expression to what is more intuitive, less determined by reason, more guided by empathy, by emotional intelligence, reflection and self-mindfulness. It is therefore more relational, both with the self and with others, thus providing an ethical basis for the urge to want to 'help others' that often underlies people's motivations to enter social work.

Allowing emotions into moral decision making has sometimes been viewed with caution because feelings have been regarded as 'transitory, changeable and capricious' (Blum 1980: 2). The rationalist and strongly principle based arguments have emphasised that in order to obtain clarity about an ethical decision we should strive to distance ourselves from what we feel, for feelings can run out of our control and lead to unjust decisions. These traditional arguments retain validity, but they should be tempered with more recent insights into the intelligence of emotions, and how this faculty of our brains can sometimes be combined with rational thought to produce more balanced moral assessments and actions. Taking this into account, even strong advocates of the use of emotion in ethical decision making such as Held (2006: 538–539) argue that 'raw emotion' must be 'reflected on and educated' if it is to be a part of our guide to morality.

Noddings (2002: 30) summarises this change of emphasis from reason to reasoned emotion when she writes that 'care theorists do not turn to logic for a categorical imperative; rather they turn to an ideal of character'. She has in mind a person who can become aware of and use emotions as well as thought, their moral motivation arising 'either spontaneously (in natural caring) or through deliberate reflection on an ideal of caring that has become part of their character' (2002: 30–31). Such a person is drawing upon what Hugman (2005: 49) terms 'complementary forms of awareness of and response to the world that support ethical thought and action'. Thus reason and feeling interact and inform one another, leading to decisions and viewpoints that are cognisant of both inner emotions and the outer, social world – a world that demands reasoned (and reasonably defensible) conduct from professional people.

Noddings acknowledges that the ethics of care are 'very close to virtue ethics' (2002: 31) which is a system of thinking in which moral motivations are seen as emerging primarily from within the actor rather than from without (van Hooft 2006). Virtues – examples of which are *love, compassion, care, genuineness, altruism* – are qualities present *in* a person, 'character traits' (Banks and Gallagher 2009), that influence or determine behaviour, including the mental behaviours of thinking and feeling. Thus, a virtue is an inner state that may be based upon emotion or thought or, more likely, a combination of both.

Such thinking and feeling lead an individual to have a personal disposition that others may see as 'characteristic' of him or her. And, over time, this disposition can lead to a *pre*disposition, a way of being that guides a person's approach to the world, becoming indelibly 'written' into who they are at the most profound level. We therefore see that virtues such as love or altruism are not behaviours that are turned on for an occasion, or attitudes that are held only because they appear in a code of ethics. Rather, they go to the depths of a person insofar as a virtuous person may feel of their own attitudes and actions that they 'can be and do no other'. This way of thinking about ethics within the person, as well as written in a code, is supported by the GSCC (2008) when they state that a person's 'suitability' for social work extends to who they are 'in work or outside work'. Suitability is thereby associated with character, and not simply with performing the role of 'social worker'.

A simple case study will serve to make the distinction between the ethics of care and other ways of thinking about ethical behaviour.

---

 **Case Study One**

Peter, aged 10, is taunted by other pupils at school. A classmate, Ashoka, feels upset about what is happening and befriends him.

We can interpret this as Ashoka demonstrating the virtues of *compassion* and *courage* because he cares for Peter and, by doing so, risks bringing the bullies' attention on to himself.

The argument from the viewpoint of the ethics of care and virtue would be that Ashoka did what he did not *primarily* because there is a rule that he should do so, or because he rationally weighed up the consequences of his actions, saying to himself, 'If I do this, this will follow.'

Rather, he did it from a 'natural caring …that arises…spontaneously out of affection or inclination' (Noddings 2002: 29).

If Ashoka's actions were emerging from his inner 'character' (rather than from obedience to an external principle of behaviour) then others might say of him, 'It's like Ashoka to do that'.

---

This case study is designed to clarify the differences between principle based ethics that are based upon the observation of codes of conduct and those that emerge through 'natural caring'. These two ways of thinking about ethics appear at first to be dichotomous but they can be reciprocal processes in that what begins as behaviour in obedience to a principle can, over time (sometimes through Noddings' idea of 'reflecting on an ideal'), become a character trait.

Therefore, the term 'character trait' should not be seen as a quality that some people such as Ashoka are born with, while others or not. Rather, character traits are formed through learning. Forni (quoted in Farsides 2007) expresses the idea like this:

> We can learn to be decent and caring; we can learn to give of ourselves; we can learn to love. How do we do that? The same way we learn how to speak, read, swim, or ride a bicycle: we need somebody to teach us, and we need practice.

Thus, character traits and behavioural principles are in a relationship of reciprocity, each capable of informing and reinforcing the other.

In what follows the ethics of care and virtues will be presented as the ethical basis of the use of self in social work, but the chapter will also show how principles remain of critical importance for the relational social worker.

## VIRTUES, THE ETHICS OF CARE AND THE USE OF SELF

The GSCC provides examples of what can be regarded as virtues. Among them are *respect, protecting others, maintaining others' dignity, honouring agreements made with others,* and *being honest.* Each of these is based upon a social worker's relationship with others but, for virtue ethics, they are also based upon the social worker's relationship with herself. Virtue ethics requires the complementarity of the *inter*personal and the *intra*personal, and is predicated on the belief that if the *intra*personal virtue is absent, then the *inter*personal behaviour will to some extent be ethically (and maybe practically) impaired. Clark (2006) makes this point when he writes that 'a professional's competence to carry out even the most instrumental tasks cannot be conveniently excised from their moral capacity and personality as a whole'.

Moral thinking like this goes back to Aristotle (384–322 BC) and, centuries later, Aquinas (*c.* 1224–1274). It has enjoyed a recent revival (see among others, McBeath and Webb 2002, Clark 2006, van Hooft 2006, Banks and Gallagher 2009) and is particularly appropriate to relationship based social work which requires an ethical system that is consistent with its own essence. That is, the ethics should take account of the uniqueness that is at the heart of interpersonal social work and the ways in which the personhood of the social worker enters into and affects professional practice and, sometimes, the practice outcomes. Thus, ethical behaviour, as well as being principle based, also emerges from the personality of the practitioner. In such a model, to practise ethically can only mean using the self because it is the self that is, to a greater or lesser degree, the root and container of the ethic. This is why ethical practice should take into account the practitioner's emotions as well as cognition and, when practised, become an expression of *who* as well as *what* the worker is. It is for this reason that a client may experience social work ethics as being *in* the social worker, intrinsic to and inseparable from the worker's personhood. Thus a worker is respectful not only because they apply principles of respect, but because they are a respectful person *in themselves.*

Virtue ethics has been developed by women and men, MacIntyre's (1985) work being in large part responsible for bringing it back into the mainstream of moral thinking. But the ethics of care has been shaped mainly by women (Slote, 2001, being a notable exception) and it has within it a gendered aspect. Gilligan (1993 [1982]) argued that while men are likely to see morality in terms of autonomous individuals responding to externally constructed laws, rights and duties, women 'define themselves in a context of human relationship [and] judge themselves in terms of their ability to care' (1993: 17). This gender-conscious emphasis within the ethics of care remains in the literature, although more recently Noddings has set out her own position in this way:

> I do not argue for women's moral superiority or for some 'natural' attribute in women that makes them more compassionate ...The basic argument is that people who are

directly responsible for the care of others (if they themselves have been adequately cared for) will likely develop a moral orientation that is well described as an ethic of care. (2002: 28)

Taking this view, becoming a caring person is more connected with having experienced care for oneself than it is with gender. That is, those who have been cared 'for' may themselves become a person who cares 'about' and 'for' others. 'Care', suggests Held (2006: 544), 'includes the creative nurturing that occurs in the household and in child care, and in education generally, and care has the potential to shape new and ever-changing persons'. In similar vein Carr (1991, quoted in Clark, 2006) suggests that virtues are acquired through 'habit formation' that originates in education and modelling by others.

Because children who have been cared for are likely to become adults who care about others does not lead to the conclusion that children who have not experienced good care cannot become caring people. On the contrary, there is much evidence to suggest that, through reflection, self-honesty and personal courage, the most emotionally wounded person can convert their wounds into a source of healing for other people (Nouwen 1979, Bennet 1987).

It also seems to be the case that a person who through time acts in accordance with externally derived principles may eventually internalise them, thus making them into part of their own character. This point is summarised by Scott Smith (2003: 28, emphasis added) who, in outlining the arguments of Aristotle and Aquinas, writes that 'people *become virtuous* by performing virtuous acts'. This is a process whereby external behaviour constructs inner, personality changes, so that, as van Hooft (2006: 11) comments, 'the virtuous person expresses who they are when they act and, in acting, they develop who they are'.

Thus, virtuous behaviour reinforces the virtuous personality, and vice versa. This is why virtue ethics and the ethics of care are expressive of relationship based practice and the use of self, for the ethic emerges from within the self that is being used. For this reason the ethic is authentic, by which I mean that it is the practitioner who is the *author* of the ethic. It is his or her *self* that is being transformed into the practical, moral activity of social work. Nothing could exemplify more strongly the use of self. We might say of such a social worker he *is* anti-oppressive rather than he *acts* in an anti-oppressive way.

Virtue ethics and the ethics of care lend themselves to relationship based social work but their primary application to unique relational circumstances makes it crucial that workers also refer to the universalising tendency of principles, thereby striking a balance between personalised service to their clients and the wider socio-legal context in which practice is happening. For example, principles ensure that the well-being of a child at risk is treated as paramount whether they live in the south-west or the north-east of Britain. Virtue ethics would work within this principle, ensuring that a virtue and relationship based social worker acts in the unique ways that are needed for 'paramountcy' to be felt as real in specific circumstances.

**Exercise One**

**Your life, virtues and care (Done alone and in pairs)**

This exercise should enable you to apply some of the ideas about virtue ethics and the ethics of care to your own life. The learning outcomes are:

1 Discovering more about particular episodes in your life when you have been conscientiously cared for.
2 Discovering episodes in your life when you have cared for *particular* others and taken their interests to heart.
3 Trying to name the virtues that have been present in these relationships.
4 Increasing your awareness of yourself as being, or having the potential to be, virtuous in your relationships – both personal and professional.

Before undertaking the exercise read, and *reflect* on, the following description of the ethics of care.

Those who conscientiously care for others are not seeking primarily to further their own *individual* interests; their interests are intertwined with the persons they care for. Neither are they acting for the sake of *all others* or *humanity in general*; they seek instead to preserve or promote an actual human relation between themselves and *particular others*. (Held 2006: 540, her emphases)

**Identifying the experience of virtue in your life**
**(The first part of the exercise is done alone)**

**Part 1**

1 Return to your LIFELINE and take plenty of time to do this part of the exercise. Note your experience of being cared for by others: family, friends, teachers, nurses, doctors, dentists, neighbours and other people – professional or not. The memory that you have may be of a small, one-off event, or something longer lasting. Think about who cared for you as a child, emotionally and physically, and times when you have been an adult in need – either emotionally or physically. Think of someone who has treated you in such a way that your best interests seemed to become temporarily their own.
2 Now, try to name the virtues that were present in the relationships and write them on your LIFELINE. Note that virtues can often be described by the use of single words such as *patience, kindness, tolerance, courage, love*…and so on. In trying to identify virtues, ask yourself if they appeared to emerge from who the other person characteristically was, as distinct from what they did.
3 Now find the times in your life when you have been the carer for another. The relationship may have lasted just minutes, or for days or years. It may have been during

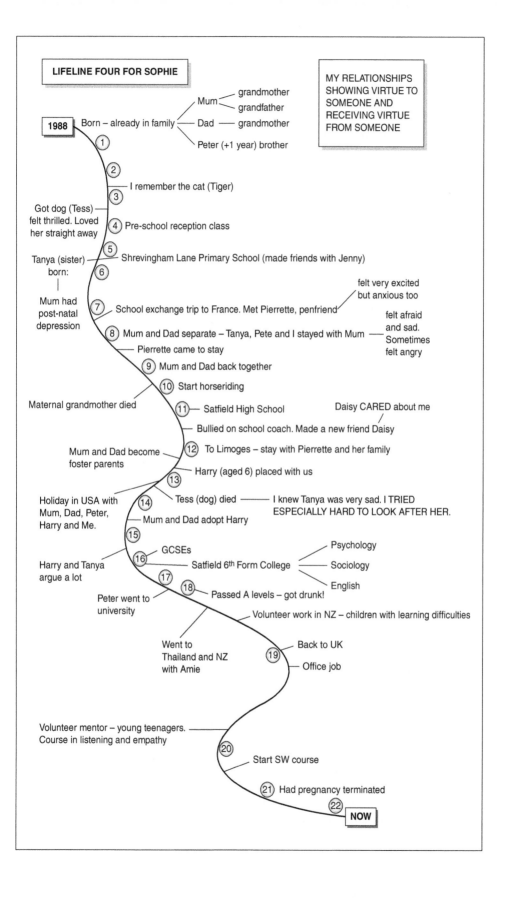

**LIFELINE FOUR FOR SOPHIE**

MY RELATIONSHIPS SHOWING VIRTUE TO SOMEONE AND RECEIVING VIRTUE FROM SOMEONE

1988

Born – already in family —— Mum —— grandmother / grandfather

Dad —— grandmother

Peter (+1 year) brother

① 

② 

③ — I remember the cat (Tiger)

Got dog (Tess) — felt thrilled. Loved her straight away

④ Pre-school reception class

⑤ — Shrevingham Lane Primary School (made friends with Jenny)

Tanya (sister) born:

⑥ 

Mum had post-natal depression

⑦ — School exchange trip to France. Met Pierrette, penfriend — felt very excited but anxious too

⑧ Mum and Dad separate – Tanya, Pete and I stayed with Mum — felt afraid and sad. Sometimes felt angry

— Pierrette came to stay

⑨ Mum and Dad back together

⑩ Start horseriding

Maternal grandmother died

⑪ — Satfield High School          Daisy CARED about me

— Bullied on school coach. Made a new friend Daisy

Mum and Dad become foster parents

⑫ To Limoges – stay with Pierrette and her family

— Harry (aged 6) placed with us

⑬ 

Holiday in USA with Mum, Dad, Peter, Harry and Me.

⑭ — Tess (dog) died —— I knew Tanya was very sad. I TRIED ESPECIALLY HARD TO LOOK AFTER HER.

— Mum and Dad adopt Harry

⑮ 

— GCSEs          Psychology

Harry and Tanya argue a lot

⑯ — Satfield 6th Form College —— Sociology

⑰ 

English

⑱ — Passed A levels – got drunk!

Peter went to university

— Volunteer work in NZ – children with learning difficulties

Went to Thailand and NZ with Amie

— Back to UK

⑲ 

— Office job

Volunteer mentor – young teenagers. Course in listening and empathy

⑳ 

— Start SW course

㉑ Had pregnancy terminated

㉒ NOW

(Continued)

your childhood (for example, caring about another child at school) or adolescence or adulthood. Again, write in words that describe the virtues that you displayed. As you do the exercise try to get in touch with the inner prompting that you may have felt, as distinct from any thought about how you 'ought' to have behaved.

**Part two**

1 Find a partner and describe to one another one circumstance when you have experienced virtue in another person, and one when your behaviour with another person has been virtuous. Name the virtues that were present in these relational transactions.
2 Are you able to frame these life experiences in terms of you and others promoting 'an actual human relationship'?
3 In discussion with your partner, each discover what you can about the extent to which these experiences have shaped your life and, perhaps, brought you to a social work career.

As with the other LIFELINE exercises you may be helped by looking at the lifeline of Sophie, the imaginary social work student (LIFELINE 4). When she was bullied on the school bus she may have experienced what felt like selfless care from Daisy. This would have been virtuous on the part of Daisy.

Sophie may remember trying to be especially kind and loving to her sister, Tanya, when Tess (the dog) died. She may have bought her a present and spent time with her. Such a way of being on the part of Sophie would be an expression of her inner compassion – expressed practically in the sister-to-sister relationship.

## THE VIRTUE OF SERVICE

The idea of social workers being the *servant* of their clients (or in the service of their service users) may be traced back to the 1930s (and probably before then). In the extract below Taft describes the servant social worker as a way of *waiting* on others:

The word 'therapy' has no verb in English, for which I am grateful; [unlike 'treatment'] it cannot do anything to anybody, hence can better represent a process going on, observed perhaps, understood perhaps, assisted perhaps, but not applied. The Greek noun from which therapy is derived means 'a servant', the verb means 'to wait'. I wish to use the English word 'therapy' with the full force of its derivation ... (Taft 1973 [1932]: 3)

This way of being, or healing, for that is what therapy means, requires waiting. Of course, waiting does not mean postponing actions that should be taken, say, to protect a child. And it does not necessarily mean waiting while time passes, for 'waiting' can often mean 'attending to', much as a waiter in a restaurant attends to his customers. Waiting, in the way that the word is used here, is a virtue because it implies constructive attentiveness, either to the self or to others. Social work examples of such waiting could be a worker attending to the impatience she feels with a client, or managing her own needs in such a way that her client's needs can emerge, or striving to remain tolerant and retain empathy in trying circumstances. And waiting can also mean giving clients time, perhaps to change, or make decisions. The process of mindfulness can also be a way of waiting on the self, perhaps for clarity to emerge with regard to the worker–client relationship.

Each of these ways of being can be seen as waiting attentively for a development, and in each action or mental state the social worker is directly or indirectly placing herself in the service of her client. This kind of servanthood is freely chosen by the social worker and is without any suggestion of inferiority that the word 'servant' can carry. The status is similar to that which was originally intended by the title 'minister', political or religious, meaning that they were 'minus' to the person being ministered to. Again, it is not inferiority that is intended here but that both the intention and the ethos of the role-holder are embodied in the role title – when acting in their professional capacity they make their personal needs and self-interests 'minus' to those of the other person.

In essence, the social worker who *chooses* servanthood as a way of practically expressing their idea of who and what they are is putting their working life at the disposal of others' needs. Understood as an ideal-type, it is an act that requires the conscious and voluntary disposition of the self for the other. And such a disposition requires the virtue of humility, because implied in being for the other is a willingness to stay close to the *humus*, or remain 'earthed' with clients and their circumstances. It is a 'self-forgetful' way of being with oneself (Philpot 1986: 149; and see as an example of humility Turner 1984), a discipline of attempting to diminish the demands made by a worker's own ego so that he or she can attend more fully to the other person.

Such a way of being sets out to give to service users what Clare Winnicott calls 'the most highly organised and integrated part of ourselves … the best of ourselves… [it] includes all our positive and constructive impulses and all our capacity for personal relationships and experiences organised together for a purpose – the professional function we have chosen' (Winnicott, C. 1971 [1954]: 11). Here Winnicott describes the social worker preparing themselves, and offering themselves, in the service of their clients and their profession.

It would help to provide a practical example of what is being said because it is important to stress the ordinariness of the social worker being a servant of their clients. It is a state of being and doing that is enacted day in, day out, in social services departments throughout Britain. The following example should help to clarify the idea.

 **Case Study Two**

**The social worker in service**

Chandrika is a social worker in a 'looked after children' team. She receives a phone call to say that a long-term fostering placement has broken down because the foster parents have, without any warning to her, abruptly separated from one another.

*(Continued)*

*(Continued)*

The child who was placed with them is Lottie, an 11-year-old girl who has physical disabilities. She requires a new placement with foster parents who are able to manage her special needs. Chandrika accommodates Lottie temporarily in a residential home, and then she begins her search for new foster parents.

During the following weeks she spends much of her time visiting prospective carers, often travelling long distances in the evening. She has felt distress about the disruption in Lottie's life, but this feeling has given way to that of wanting to do her utmost to find the right people who will be able to offer Lottie consistent care for the remainder of her childhood.

Through empathic reflection, Chandrika feels within herself the painful loss that Lottie is going through, and the anxiety and uncertainty that the child is feeling about her future.

**The virtue of service**

In this example of everyday social work Chandrika has placed herself in the service of Lottie. The feelings that underpin Chandrika's professional practice, and dedication to finding the right foster home, emerge not from rules or protocols of conduct but from her personal disposition and gift of herself to her work. It is in Chandrika's character to strive to do her best for her clients, to put herself in their service – and the eventual outcome for Lottie may spring from her use of this aspect of her character. Her actions exemplify ethics for relationship based practice – expressing the virtue of service that comes from the self of the social worker.

## OFFERING THE SELF AS A TRANSITIONAL OBJECT – ALTRUISM IN PRACTICE

In the above example Chandrika's professional behaviour was energised and motivated by an advanced state of empathy: a sensitive way of 'knowing' what it may feel like to be Lottie, and an urge to offer practical assistance. For Chandrika, the consequence was the donation of part of her life for another person – which is an example of altruistic service.

The word 'altruism' derives from *alter*, meaning 'other'. It has long been a puzzle to philosophers and psychologists why one person should help another, and what the true motives for doing so are. But the research does indicate that altruistic responses have their basis in empathy – Batson (1991: 81) claiming in his wide-ranging review of altruism that 'If there are sources of altruistic caring other than empathy, they have yet to be found.'

Empathy is a state of mind, whereas altruism is usually expressed in behaviour. While empathy is trying to feel what the other person feels, altruism is attempting to respond, often in a way that is intended to alleviate suffering. It is humane, relational behaviour, coming from an inner state of mind, and it is this that makes it virtuous and an example of the ethics of care.

D.W. Winnicott's (1958 [1951]) concepts of the 'transitional object' and 'transitional phenomena' were set out in Chapter 3. There it was seen that a child may use a transitional object to help them to manage feelings of anxiety as they involve themselves gradually with the world outside of their self-preoccupation and their mother's breast. The object, perhaps an old teddy bear, or just a piece of cloth for chewing, becomes a source of comfort, its presence relieving the anxiety that exposure to a wider world can bring. In this way the transitional object becomes part of a child's 'holding environment', existing in their mind as a symbol of safety when much else around them is changing and uncertain.

In a parallel way, a client, whether adult or child, can pass through 'an intermediate area of experience' and during this time he may use the social worker as a *human* transitional object, investing in her attributes that will mitigate feelings of insecurity while life transitions are being made. This is what a client may mean when saying of the social worker that she 'saw me through it' – where 'it' could be any form of psychosocial transition such as an elderly person moving from home into residential care, a mentally ill person being sectioned and taken to hospital, or a child moving to live with foster parents. Each of these involves psychological and social changes for the client and in this sense the person is making a transition or journey from one psychosocial position to another. These kinds of journeys may require the client to engage with a potentially painful shift in self-identity – from the sense of the self as an 'independent' person to one who is 'dependent', from a 'healthy person' to 'mentally ill', or from being a child who is 'wanted' by parents to one who is 'rejected'.

In social work situations such as these the individual worker can become an important person in the life of the client, providing them with feelings of security, a known face in circumstances that are new and anxiety provoking. But these situations may also be highly complex in psychological terms, and can cause a client to attribute qualities to the social worker that others do not see in them, and they themselves may not feel they possess. This is because the deeply anxious person may (like the children studied by D.W. Winnicott) look for a safe object, and invest in that object the qualities they need it to have if it is to soothe their troubled mind and facilitate their passage through the changes that are happening to them. At times this need may lead to distortion of reality – a distortion that will usually come to an end if the client's inner reality can grow more accepting of the reality of outside circumstances. At this time the need for a human transitional object in the shape of the social worker will diminish and eventually disappear.

In the following case study you will be helped to learn how a social worker can let the self be used as a safe or secure 'object' during a client's life transition, and discuss how reflection, mindfulness and supervised relational practice can work creatively with the emotions that are generated.

**Case Study Three**

**Situation and referral**

You are a middle-aged male worker within a city based Community Mental Health Team. You receive a referral from a hospital social worker in relation to an 18-year-old woman, Linny, who has made a suicide attempt. You are told that she was in care in another part of the UK and that she has recently arrived in your area without family or friends or permanent living arrangements. Physically, she has recovered from the suicide attempt but is assessed by the hospital social worker as 'needing practical and emotional support'.

You liaise with the local authority where the young woman was in care and you hold a planning meeting with a social worker from the leaving care team and a community psychiatric nurse. Here it is decided that you will stay involved and take lead responsibility for mental health support and practicalities such as housing.

**As the case develops**

Because Linny has been in care you are able to find her hostel accommodation and funding. You provide her with information about activities for people of her own age, help her with a benefits claim, and take her to see a careers adviser. With regard to emotional support, you arrange to see her weekly for a while and expect the contact to reduce as she finds her feet. But, instead of this, she phones your office several times a day, asking for you and not wanting to speak with anyone else. She asks reception staff for your mobile number and when they do not give it to her she says that she feels suicidal again.

When you hear this you feel concerned about Linny, and also cautious about her. There are questions in your mind such as why does she want to talk with you and not one of your colleagues, and why does she want your mobile number? How real are the suicide threats? You visit her. There is no mention of suicide, but she seems anxious. She has not made any friends and has not followed up on her benefits claim. She tells you that you are the only person she can trust.

**Reflection**

You leave Linny with no questions answered but you feel an increased level of anxiety. She appears to have singled you out as *the* person to help her. Has she idealised you? Seen you as something more, or different, than you really are? It feels as though she is not relating to the 'real' you, but to a fantasy in her mind. You decide to take these thoughts to your superviser.

**Developmental supervision**

With your superviser you analyse what is happening. You now know that Linny was in care from the age of 10, at first in a foster home and later a children's home. All contact with her family ceased around six years ago. She exercised her right to leave the care of the local authority, saying she wanted to be independent of everyone. But now, you and your superviser agree, her dominant behaviour appears to be a sought-for *dependency* on you.

Together, you and your superviser attempt to analyse her behaviour in the context of what is known about her past. The analysis of Karen Horney (1991 [1950]) comes to mind for Linny seems to be neurotically 'moving towards' you, perhaps because she perceives you as the most powerful person around her. She is also 'clinging' and you note that such behaviour can result from early insecure attachments. And, insofar as her needs are concerned, they appear to be based on 'deficiency' rather than 'being' (Maslow 1968). You also give thought to Linny's age, that she is still experiencing adolescence and the formation of identity, but instead of being able to 'let go' (Erikson 1995 [1950]) from a secure background in order to shape her own life, her emotional inheritance is one of 'identity confusion', instability and uncertainty.

Your supervision session leads to a conclusion that Linny, in coming to your city, has provoked within herself an episode of insecurity and panic which may be an emotional reliving of an earlier trauma in her life. You speculate that her acute anxiety has caused her to invest in you the quality of 'safety'. You and your superviser think about Winnicott's ideas and speculate that Linny is, unconsciously, treating you as a human transitional object who can relieve her anxiety while she undergoes the frightening experience of finding her way in the world without friends or family. If your conclusion is accurate, then you have become for Linny the central part of her 'holding environment', a symbol of security in an environment which feels unsafe.

### Resourcing supervision

Given the powerful emotions that Linny is feeling with regard to you, you discuss your own emotional resources and what you will need if you are to be 'held' during your work with her.

Your superviser reminds you that in this kind of social work *you* are the resource that the agency offers to the client, and your personhood will, for a while, be more emotionally significant for Linny than any material resources that are made available.

In your discussion it becomes clear that you should offer yourself as an emotional support, a temporary transitional object to Linny. But, while you should try to understand and engage with her feelings, you must, at the same time, avoid becoming enmeshed with her emotional world and its distortions. Retaining your self-awareness and professional role-awareness is a critical requirement if you are to avoid being drawn into her experience of reality.

To assist you in this complex emotional work your superviser recommends regular reflection, and offers more frequent supervision. Together, these disciplines will help you to know what is really happening in the relationship with Linny and the effects it is having on you. They will also enable an ongoing assessment of Linny's behaviour and whether or not it is starting to change – something that would be expected if her acute anxiety is gradually assuaged. Your superviser also asks you to be scrupulously honest with yourself in terms of what needs the relationship with Linny might activate in you. Mindfulness can be a way of discovering and naming such needs, and a way of disentangling the 'real' self from fantasy.

## LEARNING FROM THE CASE STUDY – BEING 'USED' OR THE ETHICAL USE OF SELF?

In this case we may say that Linny 'used' her social worker. Being used by another person carries a negative association. It is true that people can use each other without good coming from it and we can see such using as the basis of abuse. Likewise, one person can habitually use another as a dump for their emotional difficulties and as a strategy for avoiding the challenges of personal change.

The ethical 'use of self' means something quite different to these negative examples. It is the voluntary offering of the self as facilitator of a holding environment within which another person is making sense of and adapting to changes of circumstance or self-identity. Some people contain and manage their anxiety when facing unpredicted and undesired changes. Others may find their imagined future overwhelming and as a temporary method of management (and like the distressed child) they may use an external object (usually a person, but maybe inanimate things) as part of their coping strategy. Confused and conflicting thoughts and feelings may flow from them. They may be angry and blaming. They may be holding the social worker responsible for what is happening to them as they are, for a time, overcome by the pain and difficulty of reconciling their inner and outer worlds.

In this example Linny is using the social worker as a human resource who is helping her to pass through 'an intermediate area of experience' and to facilitate her psychological and painful transition from being a young person in care to an independent adult. The social worker becomes aware that if he decides to work with her relationally she is likely to use him as a receptor of her inner world – which could include transferred feelings from her experiences of past relationships, such as love, hate and anger, and other strong emotions.

The case provides an example of altruistic service. By using the professional resources of supervision, reflection and mindfulness, the worker has come to empathise with Linny's state of anxiety. And he turns this empathic state into practical action by offering himself to be used by her as a safe, transitional object until her experience of danger has receded. Temporarily, he took the role of servant to complement her position as service user and, most importantly, he *knew he was doing so*. Throughout the case, and by the use of supervision, reflection and mindfulness, his self-awareness remained intact.

---

### Exercise Two

**Using a transitional object or being a transitional object for another person**

In this exercise you are helped to remember or discover for the first time when you have used transitional objects in your own life, or let yourself be used as one by another person. Doing the exercise will increase your self-awareness and help you to learn to recognise when clients are treating you as a 'safe object' or transitional phenomenon.

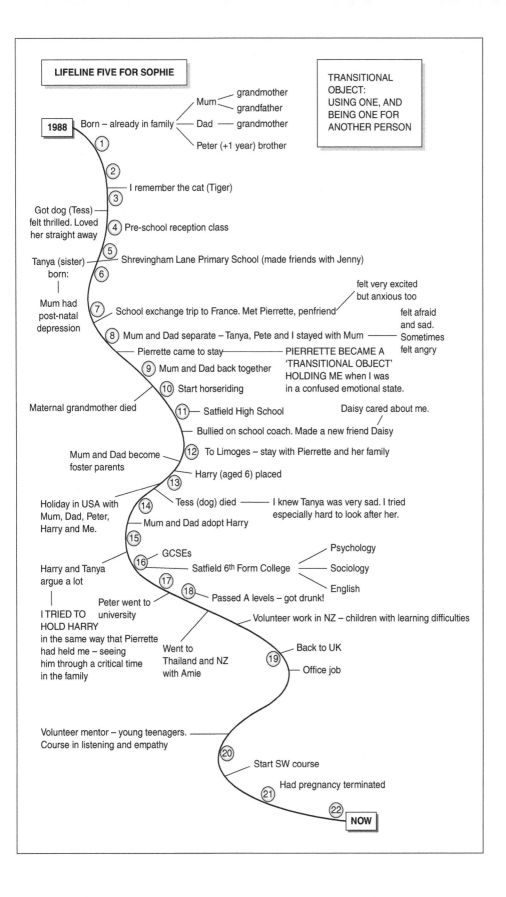

**LIFELINE FIVE FOR SOPHIE**

TRANSITIONAL OBJECT: USING ONE, AND BEING ONE FOR ANOTHER PERSON

Mum — grandmother
— grandfather
Dad — grandmother

**1988** Born – already in family

Peter (+1 year) brother

① 

② 

③ — I remember the cat (Tiger)

Got dog (Tess) felt thrilled. Loved her straight away

④ Pre-school reception class

⑤ — Shrevingham Lane Primary School (made friends with Jenny)

Tanya (sister) born:

⑥

Mum had post-natal depression

⑦ — School exchange trip to France. Met Pierrette, penfriend — felt very excited but anxious too

⑧ Mum and Dad separate – Tanya, Pete and I stayed with Mum — felt afraid and sad. Sometimes felt angry

— Pierrette came to stay —— PIERRETTE BECAME A 'TRANSITIONAL OBJECT' HOLDING ME when I was in a confused emotional state.

⑨ Mum and Dad back together

⑩ Start horseriding

Maternal grandmother died

⑪ — Satfield High School

Daisy cared about me.

— Bullied on school coach. Made a new friend Daisy

Mum and Dad become foster parents

⑫ To Limoges – stay with Pierrette and her family

— Harry (aged 6) placed

⑬

Holiday in USA with Mum, Dad, Peter, Harry and Me.

⑭ — Tess (dog) died —— I knew Tanya was very sad. I tried especially hard to look after her.

— Mum and Dad adopt Harry

⑮

Harry and Tanya argue a lot

⑯ GCSEs

— Satfield 6th Form College — Psychology
— Sociology
— English

I TRIED TO HOLD HARRY in the same way that Pierrette had held me – seeing him through a critical time in the family

⑰

Peter went to university

⑱ — Passed A levels – got drunk!

Went to Thailand and NZ with Amie

— Volunteer work in NZ – children with learning difficulties

— Back to UK

⑲

— Office job

Volunteer mentor – young teenagers. Course in listening and empathy

⑳

— Start SW course

Had pregnancy terminated

㉑

㉒ **NOW**

*(Continued)*

Again, the exercise requires use of your personal LIFELINE. You may be helped by looking at the LIFELINE of Sophie (LIFELINE 5). Her use of a transitional object may have been when Pierrette came to stay. It was soon after Sophie's parents had separated. It emerged that Pierrette had been through a similar experience, and she was able to listen empathically to Sophie and 'hold' her during a period of her life that she found frightening. In this way Pierrette 'used herself' as a way of helping Sophie to manage the new reality of her parents living apart.

An example of when Sophie may have offered herself as a transitional object concerns Tanya and her arguments with Harry. Sophie sensed that the arguments triggered Harry's feelings of insecurity about his position in the family. She may have spent time with him, listening to his thoughts and feelings and, in so doing, she may have come to represent for him a 'safe object' in a situation that he sometimes found threatening. In this way Sophie helped him to make a transition towards feeling more secure.

**Part 1 (Done alone)**

1 You are unlikely to remember what your transitional object was in your infancy, but you may have been told by your carer. It was the object that you would not go anywhere without. If you do know what it was, write it in on your LIFELINE.
2 Now think about other times in your life, perhaps of temporary emotional strain, when you relied to some extent on another person (or perhaps a pet, or an object such as your bicycle) to help you to manage external reality. Note that what is meant here is not just receiving friendly 'support' from another person. In the exercise you are trying to identify any situation when the other person or object symbolised in your mind *safety* or *security*, and you used them, and perhaps relied on them temporarily, to manage your feelings. Of course, not everyone has this experience, but do not dismiss the idea without first exploring your LIFELINE and trying to identify such a period in your life and the people around you, however short lasting and long ago the episode may have been.
3 Now think about times in your life when someone else (friend, family, or in working life) has used you as a transitional object – you becoming their *safe person*. Did you know this was happening to you? Did you let it happen, or did you resist it? Did you understand what was happening, or did it confuse you?

**Part 2 (Done with a partner)**

1 Find a partner and exchange your accounts of using a person as a transitional object, or being used by another person.

Consciously and skilfully offering the self as a human who 'sees a person through' an emotionally or practically difficult time in their life goes to the heart of altruistic, service based relational social work. It is the temporary and purposeful disposal of your professional life for the other person – requiring all the skills of empathy and emotional intelligence, and the disciplines of supervision, reflection and mindfulness. In such a practice the person of the social worker becomes the ethic in action, a human carrier of virtues.

## CHAPTER SUMMARY

- Ethics in relationship based practice go further than adherence to a principle that exists 'outside' of your self.
- Applying the ethics of care, and ideas from virtue ethics, it becomes possible to see that you, as the social worker, *are* the ethic. When you offer your self in relationship, you are at the same time bringing to your client the ethics that you carry inside you.
- The use of self can mean offering oneself as an 'object' that a client uses to assist their journey through a troubled time. Your self-offering is a virtue, perhaps of service, of love, or kindness, or courage, and a way of working that is psychologically complex, requiring a disciplined approach to self-awareness and the assistance of professional supervision.
- The chapter also made clear that the ethics of care is insufficient on its own. Relationship based practitioners must also look 'outside' and take their ethical bearings from the wider social and legal context in which they are practising. Established principles such as a child's paramountcy, anti-oppressive and anti-discriminatory practices, are of critical importance.

 *Further reading*

Banks, S. and Gallagher, A. (2009) *Ethics in Professional Life: virtues for health and social care.* Basingstoke: Palgrave.
This book (especially Chapters 2 and 3) discusses the history of virtue ethics and its recent developments. Other chapters provide examples of virtues and throughout the discussion is applied to social work and other helping professions.

Held, V. (2006) 'The ethics of care', in Copp, D. (2006) *The Oxford Handbook of Ethical Theory.* Oxford: OUP.
In this essay Held sets out her objections to ethical systems that fail to take into account emotions which lie at the heart of interpersonal relationships.

Hugman, R. (2005) *New Approaches in Ethics for the Caring Professions.* Basingstoke: Palgrave Macmillan.
Among other approaches the author discusses feminism and ethics, with its emphasis of ethics happening in interpersonal relationships.

Noddings, N. (2002) *Starting at Home: caring and social policy.* Berkeley and Los Angeles: University of California Press.
Noddings argues that social policy, rather than starting from large scale universal theory about what is 'right', should build itself on what happens in small scale situations such as a home in which people love one another.

# DRAWING THEMES TOGETHER: THEORY AND THE USE OF PERSONAL EXPERIENCE

## REVIEWING THEORY FOR PRACTICE

Social work exists as a socially organised response to people's needs and misfortunes – whether these are caused by mental or physical illness, neglect and abuse, or are simply the inequalities of society associated with social and psychological disadvantages. Social workers are called to work with clients in these kinds of states, with these kinds of backgrounds, and the central argument of this book has been that their work is likely to be more creative when it is relationship based.

The book began with a discussion of clients' views about relationships. What matters for them is not only what social workers do – a quantitative and largely measurable matter – but how they do it: a qualitative dimension that is less amenable to measurement. This quality is based upon *who* the social worker is as a person, whereas the quantitative dimension emerges from *what* they are in their role. The *what* and the *who* of social work have been recurring themes of the book – the idea and exploration of the effects that performing the professional role has upon the person of the social worker, and the influences that the person has upon the role and the outcomes of their work.

As the book unfolded you were presented with evidence about how relationships are crucial to human co-existence, for it is relationships which make 'society' a possibility. They are the glue which holds together families and communities, and this fact, that relationships are the heart of human life is what makes relationship based social work so radical. For when social workers are relational, then they are taking themselves and their work to the deepest roots of human existence.

When relationships 'work' in a positive way they are the basis of human flourishing but, as social workers know, they can also exercise destructive powers over people's lives. We saw evidence about the effects of relationships on human development – how psychology, sociology and neuroscience have shown us that personality is formed through early relational experiences, and how these experiences may have long term effects by, for example, disposing a person towards anxious or depressive responses. We also saw the effects that the loss of a relationship can have on people, and how individuals who are least connected in a relational framework are more likely to become ill and live shorter lives. This kind of relationship data has exercised a huge influence on the social work profession – in part because a holistic assessment of a client's needs will often have their relationships as its focus.

Because relationships are so important to social work's clients it is a logical step to conclude that the worker–client relationship should reflect this importance by becoming the medium and core method of effecting outcomes. In order to do this relational workers bring to bear on their relationships with clients all that is known to be most constructive of human well-being. And to understand more about how this is possible, the worker–client relationship has been considered from the different perspectives of the *inter*personal and the *intra*personal.

The interpersonal contains the emotional and cognitive transactions that take place between worker and client. Here the social worker uses fundamental relational skills and attributes. Warmth and sincerity are of basic importance, and attention was given to empathy as the method of sensing what a client is feeling, and responding in a creative manner. When empathy happens, a relationship begins. Likewise, the emotionally intelligent social worker is able to use this faculty as a method of understanding, facilitating and managing their own emotions in ways that are conducive to relational work with others.

The intrapersonal – what is 'going on inside' the social worker – has been seen as the counterpart of the interpersonal. The major theme has been self-awareness and, through discussion and case studies, the book has shown why the personhood of a social worker has such a great impact on their professionhood. The worker who knows their self, especially their emotional vulnerabilities and frailties, is infinitely better equipped to work with the emotions of others. Such a self-aware worker is emotionally poised, less likely to be taken by surprise, and more able to cope with those dimensions of practice that are emotionally challenging and, at times, exhausting.

It is for these reasons that earlier chapters of the book provided you with opportunities to become more self-aware. The relational matrix helped you to explore relationships in your own life and how significant they have been in shaping your emotional self. You had the opportunity to ponder whether your relationships are how you need them to be, or whether you would alter them if it were possible to do so. Likewise, the genogram provided a way of visually setting out your family background, and perhaps it fostered a deeper awareness of why you are as you are. Other exercises, such as the 'guided walk', helped you to sense the 'client' within yourself by placing you in a position where you were asked to trust another person.

One purpose behind exploring your inner world of feelings by use of these exercises was to help you to access and become more aware of dimensions of your intrapersonal and interpersonal life that you find difficult – because identifying these dimensions is essential preparation for relationship based social work. Perhaps the most demanding of the exercises was the LIFELINE which assisted you in tracing your social and emotional development in a chronological and disciplined manner. It facilitated you in identifying significant experiences such as loss or anxiety, and how they may continue to affect you in the present time. Again, this process is essential to self-awareness and preparing yourself for professional, relational social work.

Through exercises such as these, and through the use of literature, the book has continuously interwoven the personal with the professional – the *intra* and the *inter*-personal – emphasising that relationship based practice is *always* an interaction between these two dimensions. And a recurring theme has been that the use of self in social work requires a deep knowledge of the self that is being used. This knowledge is the core learning requirement for relational practice – where the focus of theory, practice and values falls not only on the client but also on oneself.

Relationship based social work is professionally fulfilling but it is also demanding on the selfhood of the practitioner. One cannot offer and use oneself in emotionally laden relationships without having in place mechanisms to maintain and sustain one's being. This is why the book gave attention to the personal needs of the relational social worker, needs that are often activated as a result of work. The regular use of reflection on the past and mindfulness about the present was discussed, and the discipline of developmental, resourcing and qualitative types of supervision was seen as crucial. In ways such as these (as the Social Work Task Force 2009 notes) the worker can 'review their practice and deal with the challenges and stresses arising from their work', including 'their relations with the service user'.

Like all types of social work, relational work requires a values base to guide it, providing practitioners with an ethical compass – especially in situations that present moral dilemmas. Of course, relationship based practice is rooted firmly in the principles that are common to social work, but it also locates itself within the ethics of care because this way of discerning what is best happens in 'actual interpersonal contexts'. It is an ethical system that takes into account both the cognitive and the emotional states of being, and one which places emphasis on the character of the actor. Thus, a person may be compassionate, caring, loving or altruistic – and these virtues are seen as emerging from the self rather than from a code of conduct. This distinction is important because, when ethics are *in* a social worker, they can do no other than flow naturally from that person when they use themselves for their clients.

## TAKING KNOWLEDGE, SKILLS AND ETHICS INTO YOURSELF

If you continue to reflect on the ideas and the experiences that have been generated as you worked your way through this book, then it is likely that they will gradually enter into you, influencing the cognitive-emotional framework of your mind. In this way *you* become the embodiment and the enactment of theory, skills and ethics. These dimensions of social work become encapsulated within you and realised by you.

Taking as an example Bowlby's theory of attachments, you can see that it could remain at the level of an idea, external to yourself, or it could be internalised and affect the ways in which you think and feel, and offer yourself as an attachment figure. Likewise, the skill of empathy can remain only a word used in books such as this, or it can become a practical method that you use to engage more deeply with another person. If, through study and reflection on experience, you allow intellectual ideas and practice skills to become part of who you are they will, over time, also become part of what you are as a social worker – providing a cognitive-emotional framework that you use to 'make sense' of yourself and guide what you do in relation to others.

## THE WOUNDED SOCIAL WORKER

Throughout this book you have had opportunities to think about your life and, to the extent you have chosen to, discuss it with others. In compiling your LIFELINE and genogram it is possible, perhaps likely, that you remembered some emotionally difficult times in your life. If this is the case, it is most important to stress that developing into a committed and competent relational worker is *not* dependent on what has happened in your past, but it *is* dependent on how you have responded to what has happened.

Mention has already been made of the 'wounded healer' (Nouwen 1979). It is a simple idea, though putting it into practice is demanding. The term 'wounded healer' describes a person whose ability to be therapeutic for others derives from their personal history of being 'wounded' and their courageous search to find healing. In this search they have engaged in a deliberate, disciplined and non-defensive manner with their hurts (perhaps abuse, neglect, relationship breakdowns …) and with the emotions that have resulted from these life events – especially the hard to bear feelings such as fear, hatred, rejection, jealousy and anger. Sometimes the phrase 'coming to terms' with one's life is used to describe such a person who has, often with help, brought into their consciousness the events that have pained them and emerged from this process with a feeling of relative freedom – less a prisoner of their emotional memories.

For relationship based social workers the rationale for such a deep engagement with the self is preparation for an engagement with similar emotions (and perhaps similar life events) in their clients. The process undertaken by the wounded healer can lead to a state that Tillich (1964) called 'the courage to be' – bringing a worker to the point where they have addressed their hurt state at such a level of honesty that the emotional influence it exercises over them is reduced. It is at this point that they become able to listen attentively and undefensively to their clients' pains, a situation where their own wounds have become strengths, being converted into a source of empathy and healing for others. These are social work circumstances where who the worker is matters at least as much as what they do.

## WOUNDEDNESS AND SELF-DISCLOSURE

A worker's sense of their past hurts can often bring about a greater depth of relational contact with their clients. It is a sharing that does not require words for its presence to become a constructive bond in the worker–client relationship. It is the unsaid recognition of an interpersonal link, the awareness of a common state that hardly ever calls for verbal self-disclosure on the part of the social worker. Sometimes, deep, compassionate empathy is better sensed than spoken.

And such empathy can be present even in relationships that contain conflict and adversarial elements. In settings such as prison cells and court waiting rooms, in moments of high tension such as removing a child, it sometimes remains possible to convey one's compassion for the other's plight. The process at work here appears to be the deepening of one's own sense of humanity to a level where it may touch common ground with the lives of others – even when so many aspects of their lives are different to one's own.

Such a touching *is* self-disclosure. It is of a kind that leaves the client knowing nothing about your personal life but, instead, experiencing you as a person who seems to understand, who is trying genuinely to connect in ways that are healing or creative. Thus, in relationship based social work, self-disclosure is seldom about what you say but it is always about who you are with the other person, how you dispose yourself towards and for your client.

## RETURNING TO WHERE WE STARTED: THE CLIENTS' VIEWS

All relationship based social work revolves around who you are, set within the context of social work knowledge, skills and values. And, to return to where this book started, much of the qualitative research carried out among the clients of social workers reinforces the importance of the personal in the professional. The work of Beresford and others (2008) with clients of specialist palliative care social workers makes the point. Here is one client describing the social worker:

> I can't speak any [more] highly of her because she's just fantastic really, probably the person but also the role, mainly the person. (Beresford et al. 2008)

The quotation captures much of the thrust of this book – that of the person in the role and how, in this instance, the person seemed more significant to the client.

The book has also discussed the importance of social work skills being practised most effectively within relationships. What this client says of social workers reinforces the point:

> They may have the skill but they have to bond as well, there has to be that trust and that relationship ... (Beresford et al. 2008)

Clients repeatedly say that they value the human qualities contained in social work relationships – warmth, respect, being non-judgemental, listening, treating people with equality, being open (GSCC 2008) – and such client thoughts resonate with what many social work students say: that they want to help people by working with them face to face. Clients are also reflecting one of the deepest and most natural of human impulses – that of connecting with others. Thus, relationship based social work not only provides clients with what they want, it also locates social work theory and practice within the profound human need to relate.

# REFERENCES

Adams, R., Dominelli, L. and Payne, M. (2002) *Social Work: themes, issues and critical debates* (2nd edition). Basingstoke: Palgrave.

Adams, R., Dominelli, L. and Payne, M. (2009) *Social Work: themes issues and critical debates* (3rd edition). Basingstoke: Palgrave Macmillan.

Agass, D. (2005) 'The containing function of supervision in working with abuse', in Bower, M. (ed.) *Psychoanalytic Theory for Social Work Practice*. London and New York: Routledge.

Allan, C. (2009) 'My brilliant survival guide', *Guardian*, 14 January – accessed through http://www.guardian.co.uk/society/2009/jan/14/mental-health-clare-allan-social-worker

Argyle, M. (1968) *The Psychology of Interpersonal Behaviour*. Harmondsworth: Penguin.

Argyle, M. (1987) *The Psychology of Happiness*. London: Methuen.

Argyle, M. and Henderson, M. (1985) *The Anatomy of Relationships: and the rules and skills needed to manage them successfully*. London: Heinemann.

Ash, E. (1995) in Pritchard, J. (1995) *Good Practice in Supervision: statutory and voluntary organisations*. London: Jessica Kingsley.

Banks, S. (2006) *Ethics and Values in Social Work* (3rd edition). Basingstoke: Palgrave.

Banks, S. and Gallagher, A. (2009) *Ethics in Professional Life: virtues for health and social care*. Basingstoke: Palgrave.

BASW (British Association of Social Workers) http://www.basw.co.uk/about/codeofethics/

Batson, C. D. (1991) *The Altruism Question: toward a social-psychological answer*. Hillsdale, NJ: Erlbaum.

Becker, C. (1992) *Living and Relating: an introduction to phenomenology*. London: SAGE Publications.

Beckett, C. (2006) *Essential Theory for Social Work Practice*. London: SAGE Publications.

Bee, H. and Boyd, D. (2007) *The Developing Child* (11th edition). London: Pearson.

Beitman, B. and Nair, J. (eds) (2004) *Self-Awareness Deficits in Psychiatric Patients: neurobiology, assessment and treatment*. New York: Norton.

Bennet, G. (1987) *The Wound and the Doctor*. London: Secker and Warburg.

Beresford, P., Croft, S. and Adshead, L. (2008) 'We don't see her as a social worker: a service user case study of the importance of the social worker's relationship and humanity', *British Journal of Social Work*, 38, 1388–1407.

Berger, P. and Luckmann, T. (1991) *The Social Construction of Reality: a treatise in the sociology of knowledge*. London: Penguin.

Biestek, F. (1961) *The Casework Relationship*. London: George Allen and Unwin.

Bilton, T., Bonnett, K., Jones, P., Lawson, T., Skinner, D., Stanworth, M., Webster, A., Bradbury, L., Stanyer, J. and Stephens, P. (2002). *Introductory Sociology*. Basingstoke: Palgrave Macmillan.

Blaug, R. (1995) 'Distortion of the face to face: communicative reason and social work practice', *British Journal of Social Work*, 25, 423–439.

Blum, L. (1980) *Friendship, Altruism and Morality*. London: Routledge and Kegan Paul.

Bolton, G. (2001) *Reflective Practice: writing and professional development*. London: Paul Chapman.

Bolton, G. (undated website entry) www.shef.ac.uk/uni/projects/wrp/rpwrite.html (accessed 14/02/2005).

Boyd, D. and Bee, H. (2008) *Lifespan Development*. Harlow: Pearson Education.

Britton, R. (1998) *Belief and Imagination*. Hove: Routledge.

Bronfenbrenner, U. (1979) *The Ecology of Human Development*. Cambridge, MA: Harvard University Press.

Carr, D. (1991) *Educating the Virtues: an essay on the philosophical psychology of moral development and education*. London: Routledge.

Clark, C. (2006) 'Moral character in social work', *British Journal of Social Work, 36*, 75–89.

Cocksedge, S. (2005) *Listening as Work in Primary Care*. Oxford: Radcliffe.

Community Care (2008) Online discussion: http://www.communitycare.co.uk/blogs/social-care-experts-blog/2008/01/social-work-terminology-servic.html. (accessed 27/1/2010).

Cooley, C. H. (1902) *Human Nature and the Social Order*. New York: Charles Scribner's Sons.

Copp, D. (2006) *The Oxford Handbook of Ethical Theory*. Oxford: OUP.

Crawford, K. and Walker, J. (2007) *Social Work and Human Development*. Exeter: Learning Matters.

CWDC (2007) *Supervision Guide for Social Workers*. Leeds: Children's Workforce Development Council.

*Daily Telegraph* (6 December 2008) 'Baby P effect: More children now being removed from families by social workers'.

Department of Health (2008) *Refocusing the Care Programme Approach: policy and positive practice guidance* (March).

Egan, G. (1977) *You and Me: the skills of communicating and relating to others*. Monterey, Calif.: Brooks/Cole.

England, H. (1986) *Social Work as Art: making sense of good practice*. London: Allen and Unwin.

Erikson, E. (1995 [1950]) *Childhood and Society*. London: Vintage.

Ewen, R. (1993) *An Introduction to Theories of Personality* (4th edition). Hillsdale, NJ: LEA.

Farsides, T. (2007) 'The psychology of altruism', *The Psychologist, 20 (8)* at www.thepsychologist.org.uk (accessed November 2009).

Ferard, M. and Hunnybun, N. (1972 [1962]) *The Caseworker's Use of Relationships*. London: Tavistock.

Ferguson, H. (2005) 'Working with violence, the emotions and the psycho-social dynamics of child protection: reflections on the Victoria Climbié case', *Social Work Education, 24 (7) October*, 781–795.

Fonagy, P., Gergely, G., Jurist, E. and Target, M. (2002) *Affect Regulation, Mentalisation, and the Development of the Self*. New York: Other Press.

Freud, S. (1971 [1900]) *The Interpretation of Dreams* (translated by James Strachey). London: George Allen and Unwin.

Garfinkel, H. (1967) *Studies in Ethnomethodology*. Englewood Cliffs, NJ: Prentice-Hall.

Gerhardt, S. (2001) 'The myth of self-creation', *British Journal of Psychotherapy, 17 (3)*, 329–343.

Gerhardt, S. (2004a) 'Cradle of civilisation: in order to develop a "social brain" babies need loving one-to-one care', *Guardian*, 24 July.

Gerhardt, S. (2004b) *Why Love Matters: how affection shapes a baby's brain*. Hove: Brunner-Routledge.

Germer, C. (2005) 'Mindfulness: what is it? What does it matter?' in Germer, C., Siegel, R., Fulton, P. (eds) (2005). *Mindfulness and Psychotherapy*. New York and London: Guilford Press.

Gilbert, P. (2007) 'Evolved minds and compassion in the therapeutic relationship', in Gilbert, P. and Leahy, R. (2007) *The Therapeutic Relationship in the Cognitive Behavioural Psychotherapies*. London: Routledge.

Gilbert, P. (2009) *The Compassionate Mind*. London: Constable.

Gilligan, C. (1993 [1982]) *In a Different Voice: psychological theory and women's development*. Cambridge, Mass.: Harvard University Press.

Goffman, E. (1990 [1959]) *The Presentation of Self in Everyday Life*. London: Penguin.

Goldberg, E. (1953) 'Relationship in case work', *British Journal of Psychiatric Social Work, 8, November*.

Goleman, D. (2006) *Emotional Intelligence: why it can matter more than IQ*. New York: Bantam Books.

GSCC (2008) *Social Work at its Best: a statement of social work roles and tasks for the 21st century* (2008). London: GSCC in association with the Commission for Social Care Inspection, Children's Workforce Development Council, Social Care Institute for Excellence, Skills for Care.

Harrison, K. and Ruch, G. (2007) 'Social work and the use of self', in Lymbery, M. and Postle, K. (2007) *Social Work: a companion to learning*. London: SAGE Publications.

Hawkins, P. and Shohet, R. (2006) *Supervision in the Helping Professions*. Berkshire: Open University Press, McGraw-Hill Education.

Held, V. (2006) 'The ethics of care', in Copp, D. (2006). *The Oxford Handbook of Ethical Theory*. Oxford: OUP.

Hill, T. (2006) 'Kantian normative ethics', in Copp, D. (2006). *The Oxford Handbook of Ethical Theory*. Oxford OUP.

Hogg, M. and Vaughan, G. (2005) *Social Psychology (4th edition)*. Harlow: Pearson Education.

Hoggett, P. (2006) 'Conflict, ambivalence, and the contested purpose of public organisations', *Human Relations, 59 (2), 175–194*.

Horney, K. (1991) [1950] *Neurosis and Human Growth: the struggle towards self-realisation*. New York: W.W. Norton.

Howe, D. (1993) *On Being a Client*. London: SAGE.

Howe, D. (1995) *Attachment Theory for Social Workers*. Basingstoke: Macmillan.

Howe, D. (1998) 'Relationship-based thinking and practice in social work', *Journal of Social Work Practice, 12 (1), 45–56*.

Howe, D. (2008) *The Emotionally Intelligent Social Worker*. Basingstoke: Palgrave Macmillan.

Howe, D. (2009) *A Brief Introduction to Social Work Theory*. Basingstoke: Palgrave Macmillan.

Howe, D. and Hinings, D. (1995) 'Reason and emotion in social work practice', *Journal of Social Work Practice, 9 (1), 5–14*.

Hugman, R. (2005) *New Approaches in Ethics for the Caring Professions*. Basingstoke: Palgrave Macmillan.

IFSW (International Federation of Social Workers), http://www.ifsw.org/

Ingleby, E. (2006) *Applied Psychology for Social Work*. Exeter: Learning Matters.

Irvine, E. (1966) 'A new look at casework', in Younghusband, E. (1966).

Jopling, D. (2000) *Self Knowledge and the Self*. New York and London: Routledge.

Kabat-Zinn, J. (1990) *Full Catastrophe Living: using the wisdom of your body and mind to face stress, pain and illness*. New York: Bantam Dell.

Kabat-Zinn, J. (1994) *Wherever You Go There You Are*. New York: Hyperion.

Kabat-Zinn, J. (2005) *Coming to Our Senses: healing ourselves and the world through mindfulness*. London: Piatkus Books.

Kadushin, A. (1985) *Supervision in Social Work*. New York: Columbia University Press.

Kahn, M. (1997) *Between Therapist and Client: the new relationship*. New York: W.H. Freeman.

Kanter, J. (ed.) (2004) *Face to Face with Children: the life and work of Clare Winnicott*. London: KARNAC.

Knott, C. (2007) 'Reflective practice revisited', in Knott, C. and Scragg, T. (eds) *Reflective Practice in Social Work*. Exeter: Learning Matters.

Knott, C. and Scragg, T. (eds) (2007) *Reflective Practice in Social Work*. Exeter: Learning Matters.

Kohut, H. (1977) *The Restoration of the Self*. New York: International Universities Press.

Kohut, H. (1984) *How Does Analysis Cure?* Chicago and London: University of Chicago Press.

Koprowska, J. (2008) *Communication and Interpersonal Skills in Social Work*. Exeter: Learning Matters.

Lishman, J. (2002) 'Personal and professional development', in Adams et al. (2002).

MacIntyre, A. (1985) *After Virtue: a study in moral theory* (2nd edition). London: Duckworth.

Maltby, J., Day, L. and Macaskill, A. (2007) *Introduction to Personality, Individual Differences and Intelligence*. Harlow: Pearson Education.

Manis, J. and Meltzer, B. (1967) *Symbolic Interaction: a reader in social psychology*. Boston: Allyn and Bacon.

Maslow, A. (1968) *Towards a Psychology of Being*. Princeton, NJ: Van Nostrand.

Matthews, I. (2009) *Social Work and Spirituality*. Exeter: Learning Matters.

Mattinson, J. (1975) *The Reflection Process in Casework Supervision*. London: Tavistock.

Mayer, J., Salovey, J. and Caruso, D. (2000) 'Models of emotional intelligence', in R.J. Sternberg (ed.) *The Handbook of Intelligence*. Cambridge: CUP.

McBeath, G. and Webb, S. (2002) 'Virtue ethics and social work: being lucky, realistic, and not doing one's duty', *British Journal of Social Work, 32*, 1015–1036.

Mead, G.H. (1934) *Mind, Self and Society*. Chicago: University of Chicago Press.

Milgram, S. (1974) *Obedience to Authority*. London: Tavistock.

Miller, L. (2006) *Counselling Skills for Social Work*. London: SAGE Publications.

Mischel, W., Shoda, Y. and Smith, R. (2004) *Introduction to Personality: toward an integration* (11th edition). Hoboken, NJ: John Wiley & Sons.

National Occupational Standards for Social Work (2004) Topss UK Partnership. Leeds, England (April)

Noddings, N. (2002) *Starting at Home: caring and social policy*. Berkeley and Los Angeles: University of California Press.

Nouwen, H. (1979) *The Wounded Healer*. New York: Doubleday Image Books.

Oko, J. (2008) *Understanding and Using Theory in Social Work*. Exeter: Learning Matters.

Parker, J. and Bradley, G. (2003) *Social Work Practice: assessment, planning, intervention and review*. Exeter: Learning Matters.

Payne, M. (2005) *Modern Social Work Theory*. Basingstoke: Palgrave Macmillan.

Peach, J. and Horner, N. (2007) 'Using supervision: support or surveillance?' in Lymbery, M. and Postle, K. (eds) (2007), *Social Work: a companion to learning*. London: Duckworth.

Perlman, H. (1979) *Relationship: the heart of helping people*. Chicago: University of Chicago Press.

Philpot, T. (ed.) (1986) *Social Work: a Christian perspective*. Tring, Herts.: Lion Publishing.

Postle, K. (2007) 'Value conflicts in practice', in Lymbery, M. and Postle, K. (eds) (2007), *Social Work: a companion to learning*. London: Duckworth.

QAA (2008) The Benchmark for Social Work – The Quality Assurance Agency for Higher Education.

Reder, P. and Duncan, S. (2003) 'Understanding communication in child protection networks', *Child Abuse Review, 18*, 82–100.

Robinson, Y. (1978) *The Development of a Professional Self*. New York: AMS Press.

Rogers, C. (1980 [1963]) *A Way of Being*. Boston: Houghton Mifflin.

Ruch, G. (2002) 'From triangle to spiral: reflective practice in social work education, practice and research', *Social Work Education, 21 (2),*199–216.

Ruch, G. (2005) 'Relationship based practice and reflective practice: holistic approaches to contemporary child care social work', *Child and Family Social Work, 10*, 111–123.

Ruch, G., Turney, D. and Ward, A. (2010) *Relationship Based Social Work: getting to the heart of practice*. London and Philadelphia: Jessica Kingsley Publications.

Rustin, M. (2005) 'Conceptual analysis of critical moments in Victoria Climbie's life', *Child and Family Social Work, 10*, 11–19.

Salovey, P. and Mayer, J. (1990) 'Emotional intelligence', *Imagination, Cognition and Personality, 9*, 185–211.

Salovey, P., Rothman, A., Detweiler, J. and Steward, W. (2000) 'Emotional states and physical health', *American Psychologist, 55 (1)*, 110–121.

Schofield, G. (1998) 'Inner and outer worlds: a psychosocial framework for child and family social work', *Child and Family Social Work, 3*, 57–67.

Schore, A. (2001a) 'The effects of a secure attachment relationship on right brain development, affect regulation, and infant mental health', *Infant Mental Health Journal, 22*, 7–66.

Schore, A. (2001b) 'The effects of early relational trauma on right brain development, affect regulation, and infant mental health', *Infant Mental Health Journal, 22*, 201–269.

Scott Smith, R. (2003) *Virtue Ethics and Moral Knowledge: philosophy of language after Macintyre and Hauerwas*. Aldershot: Ashgate Publishing.

Seden, J. (2005) *Counselling Skills in Social Work Practice*. Buckingham: Open University Press.

Siegel, D. (1999) *The Developing Mind*. New York: Guilford Press.

Slote, M. (2001) *Morals from Motives*. Oxford: Oxford University Press.

Slote, M. (2006) 'Moral sentimentalism and moral psychology', in Copp, D. (2006).

Social Work Task Force (2009) '*Building a Safe, Confident Future*'. The Final Report (November).

Stern, D. (1985) *The Interpersonal World of the Infant*. New York: Basic Books.

Sudbery, J. (2002) 'Key features of therapeutic social work: the use of relationship', *Journal of Social Work Practice, 16 (2)*, 149–162.

Taft, J. (1973 [1932]) *The Dynamics of Therapy in a Controlled Relationship*. Gloucester, Mass.: Peter Smith.

Thompson, N. (2005) *Understanding Social Work: preparing for practice* (2nd edition). Basingstoke: Palgrave Macmillan.

Thompson, N. (2009) *Practising Social Work: meeting the professional challenge*. Basingstoke: Palgrave Macmillan.

Thompson, N. and Thompson, S. (2008) *The Social Work Companion*. Basingstoke: Palgrave Macmillan.

Tillich, P. (1964) *The Courage to Be*. London: The Fontana Library.

Trevithick, P. (2005) *Social Work Skills: a practice handbook*. Maidenhead: Open University Press.

Turner, M. (1984) 'Arriving where we started: learning about failure in social work', *Issues in Social Work Education, 4 (1) Summer 1984*, 43–54.

Van Hooft, S. (2006) *Understanding Virtue Ethics*. Chesham: Acumen Publishing.

Ward, A. and McMahon, L. (eds) (1998) *Intuition Is Not Enough: matching learning with practice in therapeutic child care.* London and New York: Routledge.

White, S., Fook, J. and Gardner, F. (2006) *Critical Reflection in Health and Social Care.* Maidenhead: Open University Press.

Wilson, K., Ruch, G., Lymbery, M. and Cooper, A. (2008) *Social Work: an introduction to contemporary practice.* Harlow, Pearson Education.

Winnicott, C. (1971) [original paper presented in 1954] *Child Care and Social Work: a collection of papers written between 1954 and 1963.* London: Bookstall Services.

Winnicott, C. (2004 [1964]) 'Development towards self-awareness', in Kanter, J. (2004).

Winnicott, D. W. (1958 [1951]) 'Transitional objects and transitional phenomena: a study of the first not me possession', in *Collected Papers: through paediatrics to psycho-analysis.* London: Tavistock Publications.

Winter, K. (2011) *Building Relationships and Community with Young Children.* London and New York: Routledge.

Younghusband, E. (1966) *New Developments in Casework.* London: George Allen and Unwin Ltd.

Zalidis, S. (2001) *A General Practitioner, His Patients and Their Feelings.* London: Free Association Books.

Zimbardo, P. (2008) *The Lucifer Effect: how good people turn evil.* New York: Random House.

# INDEX

This index is in word-by-word order. Page references in *italics* indicate figures.